Jack Skelton-Wallace was born in Sheffield in the 1930s. He left school at fifteen and became an apprentice railway signalman, prior to National Service in the Army which, for him, was a brilliant opportunity to experience a much wider world. He later worked in the steel industry, heavy engineering and, by way of contrast, in the music business. He has also served as a soldier in the TA and, for eight years was an officer with the Army Cadet Force.

It was not until he was in his forties that he was able to pursue his lifelong ambition to study at university, reading for a BA, Double Honours, degree in Ancient History and Classical Civilisation followed by an MA in Ancient Greek Religion, both at the University of Sheffield. At that time he also undertook a study tour of Israel. Following university he lectured on Ancient Greek Society and Culture, touring major Greek archaeological sites with, and lecturing to, retired American academics. He later moved to London to work in the Institute of Archaeology and Hebrew Studies Libraries at University College London. During this time he researched a PhD which he was awarded at the age of sixty-three and is a Fellow of the Royal Geographical Society.

He has trekked from Land's End to John O'Groats twice, and also through Syria and Jordan with the author Bill Bryson, all for three different national charities. In 2001 he retired to Dorset with his wife, Enid. In the same year he founded the Wessex Highlanders Pipe Band, based in Gillingham, Dorset which after eighteen months he felt able to leave in order to undertake his second 'LEJOG' trek and spend time concentrating on historical research.

GW00601332

A Selection of

PARISH
CHURCHES

in and around Cranborne Chase,
Nadder Valley and the Blackmore Vale

North Dorset, East Somerset and South-West Wiltshire

JACK SKELTON-WALLACE

Illustrations
CLIVE FORWARD

RICHMOND HILL PRESS

First published in the United Kingdom in 2004 by
Richmond Hill Press, 11, Barleyfields, Gillingham, Dorset SP8 4UN
Email: richillpress@hotmail.com

British Library Cataloguing in Publication Data
A catalogue record for this book is available from the British Library.

ISBN 0-9548000-0-1

Cover Design by Andrea Purdie

Printed in Great Britain by Salisbury Printing Company Ltd. Salisbury.

Cover illustration: St Mary's Church, Donhead © Clive Forward

For Enid, Rowena and Andrew
and especially my fine grandsons
James Andrew John Kirton and William Edward Peter Kirton

and to parents – in absentia

AD MAIOREM DEI GLORIAM

CONTENTS

FOREWORD
by The Bishop of Salisbury
The Right Reverend Dr David Stancliffe

The parish churches of England have an integral and honoured place in the English landscape; they are a palimpsest of our history. But they are more than the focal points of a community's memory, more than the meeting-places of past and present, more than monuments or memorials to a former faith. They are sacred spaces, set apart by the people of God for worship, prayer, and encounter with the awesome reality of the divine. They offer to all who pass by a powerful and visible sign of God's abiding presence and to all who enter a transforming vision of beauty and holiness.

That presence confronts all who stumble across the treasures of Cranborne Chase, the Nadder Valley and the Blackmore Vale. I hope that those who cross the threshold and enter the sacred space within will find themselves engaged by the sense of God's abiding presence and caught up by the transforming vision of his holiness.

I am sure that this book will be an invaluable guide to those who wish to deepen their understanding of and love for these unique places. May you receive God's blessing as you reflect on his abiding presence and power.

+David Sarum

[signature] 2004

South Canonry
The Close
Salisbury SP1 2ER

FOREWORD
by The Mayor of Gillingham
Councillor Colin Dann

Our parish churches are a very visible reminder of our nation's rich, christian-based, cultural past and present. Looking around them serves to remind us of earlier generations who endeavoured to serve their communities over centuries, not only in peaceful times but through the dark days of war and personal tragedy.

Those who enjoy reading about the past will find through this work their knowledge is increased in depth and breadth. This detailed and elegantly written study with much original material will provide a profound insight into our local heritage within the Blackmore Vale, Cranborne Chase and the Nadder Valley. The author does not talk down to his reader but through his enthusiasm encourages them to undertake further personal study in many fields; architecture, stained-glass, carving, bells, monuments etc.

The charming and characterful line-drawings by local artist Clive Forward wonderfully complement the text. I hope that the work of the writer and artist will prompt readers from outside this beautiful area of England to spend some time here, to visit these rural churches and share with the inhabitants of these small towns and villages the wealth of artistic talent and spiritual presence to be found within.

Colin Dann 2004
Mayor of Gillingham
Town Hall
School Road
Gillingham
Dorset SP8 4QR

ACKNOWLEDGEMENTS

Acknowledgements are where cliché and the outstandingly obvious can, by their very nature, easily destroy genuine sincerity and the honest warmth of gratitude; I will try to avoid them. That said however, a book is the product of a number of minds, not solely that of the author. There are those who have contributed because of a personal desire for the work to succeed and others who found themselves able to help through some professional background experience and expertise. Acknowledgements are also where important omissions may be made; should there be any it is quite unintentional.

Where does one begin? I feel it appropriate (and wise) to mention my family first. It is perfectly right and proper to recognise and record that the contributions of Enid, my wife, have been enormous. I only did the research and the creative processes but she has made it possible in practical terms by typing, suggesting changes and generally encouraging. My gratitude in this and other things is, therefore, for eternity. Behind every successful writer is a damned good editor. My wonderful and gifted daughter, Rowena Skelton-Wallace, has fulfilled that professional role to perfection. My debt and gratitude to her is enormous and forever.

I am also very mindful of the willing and generous co-operation of the following: The Right Reverend Dr David Stancliffe, Bishop of Salisbury for his perfect and uplifting *Foreword* to this book; Councillor Colin Dann, Mayor of Gillingham, not only for his *Foreword* but also for his encouragement, and good and kind humour; Dr Helen Nicholson, School of History & Archaeology, Cardiff University, for her generosity of scholarship, her patience and for sharing her vast knowledge of the Templar Order, particularly in relation to Templecombe; Dr Greg O'Malley for his generosity and his willingness to share his research into the Hospitaller Order at Templecombe; Dr John Chandler of East Knoyle for his courtesy, charm and practical suggestions based on his wide experience of publishing local works; Henry Haig, a charming and talented gentleman, one of our most perceptive and sensitive stained-glass artists; Andrea Purdie of London a superbly imaginative artist and the designer of the cover of this book; Joan Salmon, yet another talented artist, based in North Dorset; Anthony Claydon of East Knoyle, Rex Sawyer of Tisbury, Peter Crocker of Gillingham, Michael McGarvie FSA and members of the Frome Society for Local Study – ladies and gentlemen all – thank you for your encouragement and good wishes; Bob Walton, ex-Gillingham Press for his friendship and myriad kindnesses; Theresa Day of Gillingham Press for her good nature, humour and generosity of spirit; James Lang, a relative of the Manger family who built St George's, Langham, Gillingham, for his information on the family; Howard Tadd of the Salisbury Printing Co. Ltd., for his advice and experience. Although Gillingham Library is small, its staff are always a delight, they are wonderfully helpful and professional in their attitude. I wish to thank, personally, each of the following: Linda Antell (Librarian), Michael Findell, Annette Lyons, Margaret Robinson, Susan Screech and Barbara Watling.

A special thank you to the compilers of church notes available in some of the churches covered. Where possible, their names have been recorded in the appropriate church text.

A special tribute should be made to the shades of Sir Nicholas Pevsner, Sir John Betjeman and Alec Clifton-Taylor; their inspiration is all.

I am grateful to the following publishers who have kindly given permission for quotations to be used:

The Random House Group – from *The Victorians* by A N Wilson, published by Hutchinson. Reprinted by permission of The Random House Group Ltd.

A & C Black – *The Victorian Church Vol.II* (1970) by Owen Chadwick.

Oxford University Press – 'Art in the Latin East 1098–1291' by J Folda from, *The Oxford History of the Crusades,* edited by Jonathan Riley-Smith (1999).

Phillimore & Co.Ltd, Shopwyke Manor Barn, Chichester, West Sussex, PO20 2PG – *Domesday Book in the Classroom* by John Fines (1982).

Sutton Publishing – *The Knights Templar* by Helen Nicholson (2001).

B.T. Batsford Ltd.(now Chrysalis Books) – *English Parish Churches as Works of Art* by Alec Clifton-Taylor (1974).

My thanks are also due to the National Trust and Dovecote Press whose books I have used as points of reference.

I have made every effort to fulfil copyright requirements; should there be any omissions or perceived infringements I apologise. Please notify the publishers if this has occurred, when the error will be rectified in future editions. For any other omissions or errors of fact I also ask for forgiveness. They are my mistakes and I stand by them.

ABBREVIATIONS AND NOTES

c. – circa

Dec. – Decorated period.

NADFAS – National Association of Decorative and Fine Arts Societies.

N./S./E./W. – Cardinal points of compass.

O.E. – Old English.

Perp. – Perpendicular period.

PRO – Public Record Office.

RCHM – Royal Commission on Historical Monuments.

All the churches covered in this book can be found in the Ordnance Survey Landranger Series 1:50,000 – Map numbers 183, 184, 194.

PREFACE

'Architecture is the only art form we can walk into,
out of, around and climb over,'
David N Durant, *Handbook of British Architecture.*
✳
'Architecture is inhabited sculpture.'
Constantin Brancusi.
✳

I have had a lifelong interest in English Parish Churches. All these churches have their own fascinating stories to tell and that, in a small way, I have endeavoured to do. They hold keys, not only to local history, but often to national and some international history. This volume covers a selection of churches from north Dorset, east Somerset and south-west Wiltshire; including parts of the Blackmore Vale, the Nadder Valley and Cranborne Chase. Gillingham and Shaftesbury are the two largest towns of the area and the other churches are found within a ten mile radius. A number of churches were chosen at random; the rest, either because they had an interesting exterior architectural aspect or a significant internal characteristic.

The accompanying text contains elements of history, architecture and furnishings together with my initial impressions upon seeing and entering a particular church. I hope this book will encourage others to seek out these churches for themselves and, perhaps, inspire them to pursue their own studies. I would like it to act as a lightly historic, aesthetic and spiritual appetizer, to stimulate the emotions of appreciation and enjoyment.

You will discover that each church has been presented in an individual manner, according to its own merits and points of interest. One of the greatest pleasures in visiting and studying parish churches is that every one of them is unique. Some are good architecturally and some indifferent. Nevertheless there will be some feature which is special to a particular church. How very fortunate we in Britain are, to possess such a heritage; a treasure trove of unsurpassing loveliness. The more churches one visits the greater the enjoyment. Physical and spiritual aspects of churches suddenly surface in one's mind and are moments of great joy in the recalling. Where known, architects, interior artists and craftsmen are given due credit. This work is not an attempt to write a definitive history of the individual churches studied neither is it a comprehensive inventory of fixtures and fittings to be found within. Footnotes, with numbered references involving constant to-ing and fro-ing, can be very tedious; therefore, any references are included in the text, for example: Clayton and Bell *(see Silton)* etc.

There is a symbiotic relationship between a church and the community which it serves; they are one and indivisible. Therefore, I have endeavoured not only to explore some of the history of a specific church but, in some instances, have included an examination of the historical background of the town or village where a church is situated. For example: Gillingham is a town with a long verifiable historical record, situated in an area where Norman and Plantagenet Kings went to reside, periodically, for the pursuit of hunting within the extensive surrounding forest; Bruton is a small town of great charm with a wealth of fine buildings and a church of great beauty and importance and the village of Templecombe has connections with the Crusades and the religious chivalric Orders of Knights Templar and Knights Hospitaller – exciting, intriguing and gripping.

The Historian, George Macaulay Trevelyan, believed that the same book should appeal to the general reader and to the student of History. Writing in the history journal, *Clio*, he remarked that, '… if historians neglect to educate the public, if they fail to interest it intelligently in the past, then all their historical learning is valueless except in so far as it educates themselves.'

We are no longer a deeply traditional society or, at least, we stand on the precipitous edge of no longer being so. Churches represent an older world, a receding world of profoundly different values. These wonderful buildings reflect, amongst other things, the religious and artistic aspirations of earlier generations; the former inhabitants of these towns and villages. They are their legacy to us; do enjoy them.

One should not forget that these churches also possess a keen active life, with a continuum of worship. They are not simply museums or repositories of fine art and craftmanship; their function is to act as a conduit between Creator and worshipper, proclaimers of the, ' lively oracles of God', as the Archbishop of Canterbury, Dr Geoffrey Fisher declared in the Coronation Service of Elizabeth II in 1953. They are refuges in times of uncertainty and doubt and a place to listen to that still small voice of calm. They are often, even now, centres of town and village life, where human personal interchange takes place.

This volume is also an opportunity to present the quite distinctive talent for draughtsmanship of Clive Forward. Clive now lives in Gillingham, Dorset but was born in Templecombe, Somerset. He was educated locally at Kington Magna, Stour Provost and Shaftesbury. A well known local figure, his work is in demand, particularly in the form of greetings cards, posters and prints of local interest. When I was searching for an illustrator, Clive, the first name mentioned, was highly recommended. This is his first venture into book illustration. I am greatly indebted to him and to Bob Walton, ex-Gillingham Press, who brought us together.

We live in an age when, sadly, theft from churches is a genuine problem and churches are rightly mindful of their responsibilities in protecting their property. However, it is annoying to arrive at a church to find it locked and lacking any indication of where one might obtain a key. This has happened to myself on a number of occasions and as a result a few churches which I would dearly have liked to include have been excluded. An individual may wish to enter a church for a number of reasons: for example, following a bereavement or other personal tragedy; or simply as a visitor, interested in churches. Many churches manage to balance the fact that theft occurs against granting access to those with a bona fide reason.

> *… As nature's ties decay,*
> *As duty, love and honour fail to sway,*
> *Fictitious bonds, the bonds of wealth and law,*
> *Still gather strength, and force unwilling awe*
> *Hence all obedience bows to these alone,*
> *And talent sinks, and merit weeps unknown;*

Till time may come when, stript of all her charms,
The land of scholars and the nurse of arms
Where noble stems transmit the patriot flame,
Where kings have toiled, and poets wrote for fame
One sink of level avarice shall lie,
And scholars, soldiers, kings, unhonoured lie.

Oliver Goldsmith – *The Traveller.*

INTRODUCTION
A brief overview

DORSET

Dorset is a county with a verdant and varied landscape of downs, heaths, coastline and secret wooded valleys. Part of the beautiful Cranborne Chase lies within the county as well as in Wiltshire. Sir Nicholas Pevsner (1902–1983), the architectural historian, considered the county famous for mansions and houses but not churches, which are generally small in size. Nevertheless, it does have a number of outstanding churches: Sherborne Abbey, Milton Abbey, Christchurch and Wimborne Minster. For many people the enjoyable secondary feature of the churches is the siting of them in the landscape; their *genius loci*. Some are built from rich and warm Ham Hill stone from south Somerset whilst others are of greensand stone from the quarries situated around Shaftesbury; in fact that ancient town is built on a large hill of greensand.

WILTSHIRE

Even a fairly casual perusal of the volumes of the *Victoria County History of Wiltshire* reveals that the county has always been a widely populated area and the abundance of archaeological remains from the Neolithic Period onwards reveals that man has had a continuous desire to inhabit Wiltshire's countryside; prehistoric Stonehenge, Amesbury and Avebury mystically and monumentally confirm that. Wool was the source of the county's wealth; three hundred and ninety mills being recorded in the *Domesday Survey of 1086*.

Wiltshire has some interesting architecture; lovely churches in fine limestone, particularly in the north and west. Chilmark's quarries were famed for fine greyish–buff stone from which Salisbury Cathedral and Wilton House were built. Sir John Betjeman (1906–1984), thought St Michael's, Mere one of the greatest churches in the whole of the county.

SOMERSET

Somerset is a county of great medieval church architecture, for example Wells, Bath Abbey, and the ruined and mystical Glastonbury; all magnificent. The county is, like Dorset and Wiltshire, possessed of an idyllic English landscape, and so many of its churches project a further depth onto that rural perfection. In particular, Somerset's ecclesiastical architectural glory is in its Perpendicular period towers, although it is by no means the only county with graceful examples; Devon, Cornwall, Lincolnshire, and East Anglia amongst others, can all justifiably stake a claim. However, surely no one can gaze on the towers of the nearby villages of Evercreech, Batcombe, Huish Episcopi near Somerton, or the town of Bruton and not be deeply aesthetically and spiritually affected. The remarkableness of Somerset towers is not their size, say against East Anglia, it is the fitting exactness of their architectural composition. Somerset is possessed of almost as many good towers as the rest of England put together.

∗∗∗

As church towers figure prominently in the area covered by this volume, it would be appropriate to add a brief section about them.

Alec Clifton-Taylor (1907–1985), a nationally renowned architectural historian and an associate of Sir Nicholas Pevsner, considered that there are four desirable architectural requirements for a fine tower, which he lists in his stimulating, *English Parish Churches as Works of Art:* '(a) The horizontal divisions should be subordinate to the vertical. (b) There should be a strong angle–buttress, for, on large towers these are of great importance, visually no less than structurally. (c) The tower should become richer as the eye moves upwards, with the horizontal divisions becoming progressively loftier. (d) The summit should be reconciled with the sky; a vital point. If the termination is too abrupt, the eye will register an uncomfortable jolt.'

In the Perpendicular Period towers reached a sublime level of perfection and the spire became somewhat extraneous. It can be seen locally that spires were intended on some towers, for example, at Shepton Mallet. The foundations of a tower can clearly be seen, capped off, rising to a height of some eight feet when it was apparently abandoned; a further indication of intent is the narrowing of the tower, recessed at the uppermost level. Symbolically the spire is indeed inspiring and aspiring, its finger reaching upwards towards the heavens. It is man's attempt to be nearer to God, the source of universal power and splendour expounded by Holy Writ.

Man, growing towards an advanced state of consciousness sought a higher contact with the Divine; literally to rise, physically, above his mortal, earthly ties. The Babylonian builders of the Ziggurat form of tower testified to that concept. Early towers were safe havens, a protection against intruders. They were also landmarks and a focus of local pride.

Inside most church towers one finds a bell or bells. F J Allen, in his scholarly, *Great Church Towers of England*, draws the reader's attention to the misuse of the word 'belfry', the generally accepted name for the bell-chamber of the tower. The syllable 'bel' has no connection with the English word bell. It is derived from Old French, *belfrei* (Mod.French – *beffroi*), which in turn is derived from Middle High-German *berc frit*; *berc* – to hide, and *frit* – security. Therefore, the likely meaning is a safe hiding place or covered security.

The building of magnificent church towers minus spires possibly signifies, theologically, a somewhat less transcendent attitude, noticeable in the long recovery period following the Europe-wide pandemic of the Black Death plague. That is, Western Christian culture tended to accept the belief that the individual is only part of a transcendent whole; an infinitesimal fragment making up the universe.

Out of a total of thirty-four churches in this volume, twelve are dedicated to St Mary the Virgin. The passionate devotion to St Mary increased and grew rapidly in the Late Middle Ages, during and following the Black Death plague. Having experienced profound grief, as the mother of Jesus, she was perceived to be in a unique position. As the *Mater Dolorosa* she could act as intercessor on behalf of those who had lost family and friends, especially children. Eamon Duffy in, *The stripping of the altars. Traditional religion in England 1400–1580*, quotes a popular prayer from post-plague England, the *Obsecro Te* (beseech you earnestly):

> *Mother most glorious ... consolation of the desolate ... every hour and minute of my life ... by that great and holy compassion and most bitter sorrow of heart which you had when Our Lord Jesus Christ was stripped naked before the cross ... And by your Son's five Wounds, and the sorrow you had to see him wounded.*

BATCOMBE
– East Somerset

North of Bruton, off the B3081 Bruton
to Evercreech Road. O.S.Landranger 183.

Dedicated to
Saint Mary the Virgin

And did those feet in ancient time
Walk upon England's mountains green?
And was the holy Lamb of God
On England's pleasant pastures seen?

William Blake never visited Batcombe but his mystic and fertile imagination brought him here, to a prospect such as that observed from the S. porch of the church, looking out at the verdant rolling hills and the woods surrounding this beautiful English rural village, on a hot and shimmering day; that wonderful smell of summer England, every subtle nuance of it, hanging and dripping on the senses in the dancing sunlight.

The church notes state the topographic position superbly; 'Batcombe is a place of hills, and from whatever direction you come to it, you will see the church tower on the rise before you. It is a beautiful position for a church.'

For those visitors endeavouring to find a continuity of building styles and materials they had better commence with one single stone remaining from the Norman period; part of the outside wall of the S. aisle, which comes with the characteristic Norman embellishment of a zig-zag pattern.

The chancel of the Dec. period, the second stage of the development of English Gothic style, is now square ended and, suggest the notes, was probably a replacement for the apsidal Norman version. It is also likely that there was further rebuilding around 1700. The plain glass in the S. windows is from King's College, Cambridge, and the coloured inserted fragments are fourteenth-century.

The rebuilding of the nave in the years 1450–1500 follows that long period of social, economic and traumatic upheaval wrought by the European pandemic of the Black Death plague. After that terrible period, economic expansion gathered pace and social confidence and stability returned. It was in this period of growth that the church of St Mary the Virgin, along with many others in England, was rebuilt. The nave was increased in height and the clerestory and arched windows were added, as were the N. and S. aisles.

The church notes tell us that the walls and the sides of windows are decorated, in some places, with murals and texts; most are covered over with a lime wash which was applied for the sake of preservation. However, one small area has been left uncovered in the E. wall S. aisle. Many churches have, in the fairly recent past, discovered overpainted murals on their walls. Once the very idea of the sanctity of God's House had been breached under Henry VIII with his barbaric and wanton destruction of the monasteries, the so-called Dissolution (which makes it sound so much more refined), then his cold hearted and narrowly pious zealot of a son Edward VI (1537–53) was happy and well disposed to continue his father's work. A Royal Injunction decreed in 1547 that, '... they shall take away ... all other monuments of feigned miracles, pilgrimages, idolatry and superstition; so that there remain no memory of the same in walls, glass windows or elsewhere in the churches or houses.' A large number of churches complied, and if the windows, for example, were not broken they were taken down and replaced with white glass. Immediately following the Accession in 1558, of Elizabeth I, an Injunction of 1559 instructed Town Councils and churches to, '... remove all signs of idolatry and superstition.' Therefore, they had to cover their much loved paintings, after the Old Faith had been outlawed. Deep anguish was caused in communities when they were thus forced to shred vestments and participate in the vandalism of their own churches. The purpose of the paintings and the stained and painted glass windows was to instruct and edify. It was those symbols which linked the then present to their familial past; their grandparents and beyond. The past was forcibly obliterated from history. However, beware the zealot in an assumed official guise, often brandishing a piece of paper; it all started again with Cromwell and his iconoclasts.

The tower, 87 feet high, was certainly under construction in 1540; primary documentary evidence for that date is provided by Will bequests. The style of the tower relates it to Chewton Mendip, built at the same time and probably by the same designer. The composition of the sculpture on the W. face of Batcombe is similar to Chewton Mendip but the latter has a taller tower; 119 feet to the pinnacle tops. Batcombe with no pinnacles ends abruptly, giving strength to the Art Historian Alec Clifton-Taylor's dictat that aesthetically towers should not come to an abrupt stop causing the eye to jolt. *(See Introduction.)* A special sculptural feature of the W. face is that of Christ attended by three pairs of angels.

In 1539, possibly the year the tower at Batcombe began to rise, nearby Witham Friary, the first Carthusian monastic house in England, saw the reverse process of being Dissolved, along with five hundred and sixty other establishments in England, by order of that great royal monster Henry VIII.

In England's green and pleasant land.

BOURTON
– North Dorset

North of the A303(T). O.S.Landranger 183.

**Dedicated to
Saint George**

Bourton, intersected by the River Stour flowing south-east, stands on the boundary of Dorset and the boundaries of Somerset and Wiltshire. Erected on what is now a golf course, on the north side of the village, is the large County Boundary marker stone, reputedly placed here by King Egbert originally, to mark the limits of administrative districts of ancient Wessex. Bourton is also geographically placed half way between Stonehenge and Glastonbury; a symbolic bridge between the ancient religions and Christianity.

It is likely that there were two settlements, West Bourton and Bourton. The west of Bourton is still, to some degree, a separate agricultural hamlet. Dorset, Somerset and Wiltshire were further linked through the textile industries of those same counties, which flourished in the early eighteenth century. Yarn was imported from Holland to supplement locally grown flax. By the close of the eighteenth century, weaving was the predominant occupation; three quarters of Bourton's population were engaged in the trade by 1811. The first mill was established in 1720 and others were built early in the nineteenth century. The River Stour was highly relevant to the weaving trade; it was the main source of power. One of the water wheels was sixty feet in diameter, making it one of the largest in England. Trade, however, declined by the late nineteenth century, due to the well organised and powerful competition from the north of England.

According to the church notes based on Doris Moore's *Footsteps from the Past – a Dorset village*, there was no church here in Bourton, it being part of the Parish of Gillingham, the vicars there being responsible for its spiritual wellbeing. In 1650 the village petitioned to be united with Silton but the latter rejected the approach giving the reason that Bourton was too large and their church too small. It was not until 1809, during the celebrations of George III's accession, that a proposal was made to build a church in the village. The response was immediate, for by St George's Day 1810, the foundation stone was laid, and in 1813 the Bishop of Bristol consecrated the Chapel, which was probably already in practical use by 1812. This first chapel was very small and by 1837 it was lengthened. It is suggested by Pevsner that the wide nave of the first chapel was lengthened in 1837–8. Further work was carried out by Ewan Christian in 1878, (he also worked on Piddlehinton [1867] and Piddletrenthide [1880]). Charles E Ponting *(see Gillingham)* of Marlborough, Diocesan Architect of Salisbury, designed the attractive W. tower, with a somewhat higher stair-turret and decorated bell-stage, which is of 1903–5. (Ponting's great work is St Mary's, Dorchester.)

The interesting W. window, dedicated to the memory of General Charles George Gordon of Khartoum, donated by the Revd Benyon Batley, has an uplifting and spiritual Victorian moral tone which is hardly surprising, given General Gordon's character and the high estimation afforded him by the Victorian public.

The polygonal apse is appealing to the eye. There are a total of seven lights, all with painted and stained glass, two of which, *c.*1878, (Nicholas Pevsner claims) may possibly be by Charles Eamer Kempe (1834 –1907). *(See Donhead St Mary.)* All the windows in the sanctuary, beyond the altar rails, are Victorian and, noting Pevsner's remarks regarding Kempe, neither of the two most likely windows bear Kempe's signature. Due to Kempe's success there were a number of copyists of his distinctive style. In the simple chancel the direct focus is on the small altar and the equally simple cross, strongly projecting its challenging message.

BRUTON
– East Somerset

On the A359. O.S.Landranger 183.

Dedicated to
Saint Mary the Virgin

That remarkable lady traveller, Celia Fiennes *(see Mere)*, wrote in her Journal, for the years immediately before 1687, that she passed through Bruton on her way from Queen Camel to her home in Newton Tony, Wiltshire. 'We came by Bruton, a very neate stone built town … with four horses and a chariot, my sister self and maid thence to Willding.' *(Wylye?)*

Celia Fiennes had more to say about the wider area, but her observations about the town are interesting. She would recognise some of Bruton even now. Bruton, for those who have not visited here, is a town where the architecture is of such quality and longevity that to have one commercial building totally out of harmony with the rest of the town centre, would be an affront in many directions. There is generally some interesting domestic architecture. Ignoring, if possible, the ancient buildings on the High Street, the shops are loosely frozen in the 1950's. There are no concessions to chains or franchises.

In fact there is so much 'Architecture' in Bruton, a town of great historical significance and interest that to even attempt to describe it all here would be impossible. Therefore, the man to whom I am generally indebted is Sir Nicholas Pevsner, the architectural historian. His *Buildings of England – South & West Somerset* is essential to understanding the architecture of the town. For an excellent wider view of the town's past with photographs, *A Bruton Camera* by local writer Colin Clark, is available from the well arranged Museum on the High Street, where incidentally, there is a scale model of Bruton Church.

The River Brue, (*brue* – a word of Celtic origin meaning brisk, vigorous) runs into the town from the east, towards Glastonbury, and bisects it; on the north bank is the town centre and High Street, on the south, Bruton Church, King's School and a thoroughfare sounding like a magic spell – 'Plox'! (Possibly from the latin *ploxemum* which relates it to wagons?). Whilst another lane, running past Sexey's School, with a more down to earth name is simply called 'Lusty'. In 1638 Hugh Sexey, a Queen's Auditor, founded a hospital and alms houses of which some buildings are still extant. Sexey's School was built in 1891; a continuation of Hugh Sexey's Foundation. The School and the Foundation still flourish.

For centuries the woollen industry was a large part of the local economy and the swift flowing Brue essential to the trade. The Brue and locally obtainable fuller's earth, were both necessary elements in the washing and fulling (or toughening) process; hence – a fulling mill. 'Somerset's great churches were built on the backs of sheep,' might have been an old west country saying. Wool really was the driving force for much of the Wessex counties' economies; including those of Wiltshire and Dorset. Colin Clark states, ' … the right to have a mill on the Brue probably dates back to Saxon times although a Charter granting the right to have a mill to John le Gaunt dates from 1290.' Only one now exists in the town, Gants Mill, no longer connected with the past woollen industry, as it produces animal feeds.

Immediately before Plox, on Silver Street, is a majestic row of wall buttresses, the remains of an Augustinian Priory founded in 1142, becoming an Abbey in 1511–1536. Also on Plox, occupying a fairly widespread area, is the well known King's School, Bruton, founded in 1519 by a triumvirate comprising Bishop Fitzjames of London (born at Redlynch), Abbot Gilbert and Dr Edwards, Chancellor of St Paul's Cathedral. According to Pevsner the buildings are largely nineteenth-century but there are residual elements from the sixteenth century and further elements from the eighteenth.

The scribes of The Domesday Survey of 1086 variously described Bruton as, *Brauetone, Briweton, Briwetone* and *Brumetone*, the land being owned by King William, Roger de Courseulles (twentieth largest landowner after the King), Turstin Fitzrolf (thirty-fifth) and Walter de Douai (twenty-third). The entries show considerable holdings of some extent.

St Aldhelm (*c.*AD639–709), Bishop of Malmesbury, a man of great scholarly ability and energy, was consecrated Bishop for the area west of the Forest of Selwood. Aldhelm was responsible for the development of the West Saxon Church and, allegedly, instrumental in building an early church in Bruton. William of Malmesbury (*c.*1090–*c.*1143), educated at Malmesbury Abbey, became a prominent historian of his period. One of his great works, *Gesta pontificum Anglorum* (Exploits of the English Bishops), contains numerous anecdotes (not always reliable sources for historians). In this volume he relates a tale of how Aldhelm brought back a marble altar from Italy on the back of a camel in the year AD690. On the journey the marble cracked, but Aldhelm repaired it. The altar was given to King Ine of Wessex (d.*c.*AD726), who was believed to have been the builder of Glastonbury Abbey. King Ine placed the altar in Bruton Church and William states that he could see the crack four hundred years later.

The Romans left some of their occupational remains in the form of bronze statuettes, almost certainly votive offerings, discovered in 1960 on nearby Creech Hill where it is believed there was a shrine. The figures, which were widely popular in the Roman world, are well known and easily identifiable as Mars, Hercules, Mercury, Minerva and a priest of a Roman cult. Part of a Roman road, discovered near Godminster Wood, is believed to have run past a villa at nearby Discove (a *Domesday* entry) to Creech Hill where the shrine was situated. An interesting word, 'Discove'; is there a local explanation for this unusual name, or any connection with *disco*, from the Latin, 'to learn', bearing in mind the Creech Hill religious site and the votive offerings? Perhaps the shrine was oracular; with anxious enquirers bearing votive offerings seeking an answer to a personal problem: 'Will my baby be born healthy?' or, 'Will I be lucky in love?' and so forth. The priest of the cult would then interpret the answer given by the local god or goddess.

Such is the grandeur of the church of St Mary the Virgin that a number of well known church and art historians have been moved to eloquent description:

> *One of the proudest churches of east Somerset.*
>
> Sir Nicholas Pevsner

> *The west tower is distinguished even in Somerset.*
>
> Sir John Betjeman

> *Somerset (including Bruton) merits the first place among the English counties for parish churches considered as works of art.*
>
> Alec Clifton-Taylor

> *… a fine church tower in a classic Somerset setting.*
>
> Simon Jenkins

> *In two hundred years the people of Bruton gradually transformed the small early structure of their ancestors into the noblest church of east Somerset.*
>
> A K Wickham

It is the fame not only of the west tower but the outstanding beauty of the interior of the church which brings the many visitors to St Mary's and to the town. The church has the added distinction of possessing two towers. The main tower, built around 1480 to possibly 1490, standing 102 feet in height, is of Doulting stone from nearby Shepton Mallet. Much of the town is also built from the same fine stone, as is Wells Cathedral. At that height it somewhat dwarfs the other tower alongside the N. aisle of the nave, over the N. porch. Nevertheless, approximately one hundred years older than the main tower, the latter would grace any other Somerset parish church in its own right. According to the church notes, the N. tower was used for weddings. In the middle ages couples were met at the porch to be asked if they wished to consent to the marriage taking place. Only then would the procession enter the church for the ceremony.

Frank J Allen in his, *The Great Church Towers of England*, thought Bruton the earliest of the east Mendip group of church towers. That is, a group of church towers with similar architectural characteristics for example, Batcombe, Evercreech, Weston Zoyland and Bishop's Lydeard.

To see both the exterior and the interior in all their architectural glory, choose a bright sunlit day and time enough to enjoy them. Your effort will be well rewarded. The W. tower needs to be viewed from all angles to fully appreciate the imagination and artistry of those who had the vision to build it. Its restrained and refined elegance will delight and lift the dullest of spirits.

The beauty and harmony of the main tower is somewhat diminished by the lack of figures in the five niches on the W. face; three at the second stage and two at the third, on either side a two-light window. Whether it was intended that the niches remained unadorned, which is hard to reconcile noting other Somerset tower refinements, or whether they were desecrated by Parliamentarians is unknown. The corner, set-back buttressing arrangements are particularly eye-catching, complete as each buttress is with a detached-from-the-tower crocketted pinnacle. The four corner pinnacles are similarly treated rising well above the ornate shield and quatrefoil decorated parapet at the final chamfered and recessed battlemented stage. The bell-stage too is handsomely arranged with three pierced openings of typical Somerset tracery on each face. This arrangement is different on the N. side because of the stair-turret in the angle of the tower and the N. aisle. The bell-openings are separated by engaged stone shafts, each having its own crocketted pinnacle. The W. door, now the main entrance, is wide and high with nicely carved spandrels and hood moulding above to deflect rain water. Above is the large W. window with six lights each at the bottom and central stages and straightforward Perpendicular tracery at the upper. The tower houses a ring of six bells; the earliest dated 1528.

According to the illustrated information sheet, published by Friends of Somerset Churches and Chapels, there was an earlier church. However it was not necessarily on this same site, but wherever, it was possibly the one referred to by William of Malmesbury.

Anyone familiar with the churches in southern Germany or French palaces will recognise the rococo style of the chancel. It is difficult to be indifferent to this aspect of Georgian period architecture in England which, in the rebuilt chancel of 1743, is in extreme contrast to the Gothic nave; flamboyant and theatrical, having a wonderful rhythm in its ornamentation, showing instruments of the Passion and the sacraments. It is a sparkling Handelian flourish for soaring trumpets in a visual form (whose *Messiah* incidentally, had its first London performance the year the chancel was rebuilt; George II was on the throne and England was enjoying a period of great national prosperity).

Rococo, whilst essentially French, possessed a strong Italian influence and lasted from around 1720 to 1770. The name derives from *rocaille* and *coquille* (rocks and shells); a common motif. It is further characterised by 'C' and 'S' curves, swags, garlands and exuberant tracery. The style saw its beginnings in fashionable man-made grottoes. It was an artistic reaction against the formal Palladian style. The fundamental design of the chancel was by Nathanial Ireson of Wincanton, a local architect and builder who also built the tiny church at Redlynch.

In St Mary's there is no E. window, the entire wall is filled with gloriously gilded Corinthian capitalled columns, placed either side of a gilded framed panel of cerulean blue with a central golden sunburst glory surrounding an IHS monogram. At the extremities are gilded capital pilasters, on either side of panels of gilded rococo decoration. Above all, in the pediment of the whole classical facade, are the arms of the Berkeley family. The groin vaulted chancel roof is in the same style, the ribs richly decorated. Rococo was never a major influence on architecture in England; here at Bruton is one of the few opportunities to see this scintillating style. The facade was most likely designed by the architect James Gibbs (1682–1754), a friend of Sir Christopher Wren, who trained partly in Italy. He designed many famous buildings, one of them being St Martin's-in-the-Fields in Trafalgar Square, London. The actual work on the rococo facade was probably carried out by members of the Italian family of Artari, the best *stuccatori* of their day, who were working in England from the 1720s onwards. The church notes inform that the chancel, '… narrowly escaped being swept away by Victorian restorers.'

Beneath the chancel is the crypt which houses leaden coffins of the Berkeley family. On the N. side of the chancel, set deeply into a niche is the splendid tomb-chest memorial of Sir Maurice Berkeley, Lord of the Manor of Bruton (1506–1580), Standard Bearer to Henry VIII, Edward VI and Elizabeth I. His undamaged effigy is depicted clad in knightly armour, lying between his two wives, all three in perpetual married bliss. Katherine Blount (d.1559), and Elizabeth Sands (d.1585), are both beautifully dressed, with elegant starched ruffs. In front of the tomb is the neat arrangement of Berkeley family pews intended for use by those who have not yet gone before. Another Berkeley, Sir William, was despatched to take the post of Governor of Virginia in 1639. He, with another Brutonian, Thomas Ludwell, established one of the first Episcopal communities in America.

The Neo-Georgian rood-screen by the architect W H Randoll Blacking of Salisbury, a former pupil of Sir Ninian Comper *(see Witham Priory)*, separating the nave from the chancel, was erected as recently as 1938 in memory of Roland T A Hughes, a local solicitor and choir master who is buried in Malaga where he died. The screen is striking in its simplicity, with slender Corinthian capitalled columns and a Holy Rood with an ornate cross and polychrome figures situated on the cross member. The elegant screen and exuberant chancel are in perfect harmony, one complementing the other.

A number of other memorials grace the chancel of which the bronze on the S. wall, to William Godolphin (d.1636), third son of Sir William Godolphin of Godolphin, Cornwall, is particularly handsome and pays tribute to, '… his many virtues and good life.' It has been severally conjectured that it could be a work by Hubert Le Sueur (*c.*1580–*c.*1670), who was born in Paris and moved to England around 1628. Le Sueur, 'the French Raphael', was greatly patronised by the court of Charles I and his best known work, cast in 1633, is the statue of that king in Trafalgar Square.

The nave was rebuilt shortly after the tower; Pevsner and the church notes suggest around 1506–1523. It was then when the wide four-light clerestory windows were added. The roof beams are particularly outstanding and, on the easternmost, traces of colour still remain. The beams are supported on shafts with decorated niches; statues were added in the nineteenth century, at the same time as the fan-vaulting inside the W. tower.

St Mary's has some fine stained and painted glass. In the N. aisle, W. end, is a depiction of Christ as *The Good Shepherd*, a theme beloved by the Victorians. At the NE end of the same aisle is another Victorian window signed by W F Dixon, pinxit *(painted this)*. William Francis Dixon (1848–1928), was a pupil of Clayton and Bell *(see Silton)* and continued, after he left that company, to extend the styles he had learned. His broad developed style shows elements from the rococo to Aubrey Beardsley-ish figures. In 1894 he left London to work for Mayer of Munich. The S. aisle,W. end, window of 1889, by the Royal Stained Glassworks, Old Windsor, Berks. (established 1878), uses an interesting palette of pastel hues. The Royal Stained Glassworks had, as one of its founders (if not *the* founder), Princess Louise, Duchess of Argyll (1848–1939), the fourth daughter of Queen Victoria. The Princess was a very gifted artist, probably the most talented of all Queen Victoria's children. She lived in Kensington Palace and turned part of her apartments into a centre for art. A Fellow of the Royal Society of Painters in Watercolour, she also wrote articles for artistic magazines, under the name Myra Fontenoy. Trained in the plastic arts under two teachers, one of them being Sir Joseph Boehm, she sculpted the monument to her brother-in-law, Prince Henry of Battenburg in Whippingham Church, Isle of Wight and the life-size seated figure of her mother which stands outside Kensington Palace. She was cremated at Golders Green Crematorium and her ashes buried at Frogmore, Windsor Great Park. The W. window – *Our Lord in Majesty* – by Clayton & Bell, a culmination of the Victorian restorations, is outstanding both in size and quality. The centre row of lights depicts biblical figures and English martyrs, and the lower lights represent patron saints of England and two figures from the period of the building of the church.

The N. aisle has the royal arms of Charles II and the church notes, using primary evidence of the Parish Registers (which commence 1554), attest that both Charles I and Charles II stayed in Bruton and attended divine service in St Mary's. The aisle chapel is a memorial to King's School boys, dedicated to, in the words of the classical Attic Greek inscription on the header of the Roll of Honour, 'Those who have passed to death,' during WWI. Behind the altar is a small polychrome carved figure reredos; a very fitting addition to this poignant corner provided for contemplation by those who care about such heroic sacrifices made in the, 'War to End All Wars.'

BUCKHORN WESTON
– North Dorset

Off the B3092, west of Gillingham.
O.S.Landranger 183.

Dedicated to Saint John the Baptist

What the population of twenty-six, including five slaves, of Buckhorn Weston did during the evenings following a hard day's ploughing of the land belonging to the Count of Mortain, (*Domesday Survey* of 1086) is irrecoverable. Could those Saxons have sat quaffing ale in a rustic hostelry here, in the village centre, opposite an equally rustic church?

However, what was the *actual* total population of Buckhorn Weston in 1086? The simple statistic of 'twenty-six including five slaves' only accounts for the men; women and children were not entered into the survey. Take an average size family of four-and-a-half people and multiply it by twenty-six and the population swells considerably to one-hundred and seventeen. The population in 2003 was three-hundred and thirty.

Count Robert of Mortain took his name from Mortagne in the department of La Manche, Normandy. He was half brother of King William, fought at Hastings and became the largest landowner after the King. The Count's estates were largely in the West of England, in fact most of Cornwall was his. Mortain was a well known despoiler of the church and became involved in a rebellion in 1088 as a result of which he was banished and had his lands confiscated. Mortain died in 1090.

The Domesday Book, '… reveals some astonishing facts,' writes John Fines in his work *Domesday Book*, a guide to interpreting and understanding King William's survey. 'In 1086 the value of England was some £73,000 of which the King took for his own usage some £11,000. This was about 15 per cent and twice the amount Edward the

Confessor had … Robert Count of Mortain and Bishop Odo of Bayeux shared 7 per cent. … the Church took 26 per cent. … It is instructive also to see where the money came from: **44 per cent came from Wessex**, 17 per cent from E. Anglia, 15 per cent from W. Mercia … the poor ravaged areas of Yorkshire and Lancashire provided a bare 1.6 per cent.' The 44 per cent from Wessex, a very large territory, is nevertheless an interesting statistic and reveals a great deal about the wealth of the area.

What a splendid setting for a church; at the centre of its village, and opposite a delightful and friendly public house, the Stapleton Arms; a contemplative combination. A very solid and handsome church. The nave and chancel are of fourteenth-century origin, with later additional building in the nineteenth-century. According to the church notes, by Jeanne V Kehoe (1966), a church existed here and was well established at the beginning of the thirteenth century; a list of incumbents, displayed in the church, verifies that.

The N. aisle having an arcade of three arches, was largely rebuilt in 1870, designed by G R Crickmay (1830–1907) who was also responsible for the school building next to the church around the same time. (Crickmay also designed Holy Trinity church, Weymouth in 1887). The restoration of St John's was made possible by the Lord of the Manor, Sir Francis Stapleton. The low W. tower, with battlements, pinnacles and simple bell-stage light-openings was built in 1861. There is a ring of six bells, the earliest being sixteenth-century, and the clock – a memorial to the local fallen of WWI.

Internally, beneath the tower, are six painted, late seventeenth-century panels, depicting Old and New Testament subjects including, for example, the Nativity, King David, saintly figures and angels with trumpets. These panels, which are interesting but certainly not high art came from the front of the W. gallery when it was demolished. The stained-glass of the E. and W. windows is Victorian.

The most important monument, on the N. wall of the chancel, is that of a recumbent, unarmoured and fashionably dressed gentleman of the late-fourteenth-century, possibly a Yorkshireman, Alexander Mobray, who allegedly died here. He is clothed in short tabard, tippet and hood, tight hose and belt with purse.

The S. porch of greensand stone is genuine fourteenth-century and lists at a crazy angle due to subsidence. The niche above the doorway has an eroded and damaged statue, possibly of St John the Baptist; the vandalism, most likely, by courtesy of Cromwell's Parliamentarians.

CHILMARK
– South-West Wiltshire

On the B3089, west of Salisbury.
O.S.Landranger 184.

Dedicated to Saint Margaret
of Antioch

Situated in the Nadder Valley,
on the northern edge of
Cranborne Chase, is Chilmark
(meaning a boundary pole) in
a still thinly populated, totally rural area. Long famed for its quarries,
from whose delicate grey Jurassic oolitic limestone grew Salisbury
Cathedral, as did Wilton House, at Wilton near Salisbury. The village
is bisected by the main road and on the south side, below the church
is, surely, some of the handsomest and cosiest domestic architecture
in England; it is outstanding. There are so many facets of these
particular stone gems to be taken in that a visit here is both an ocular
treat and exercise!

St Margaret of Antioch, a saint whose name will probably not
spring readily to mind, has a number of churches dedicated to her.
She is, unfortunately, almost certainly an apocryphal figure.
According to legend she rejected marriage with the Prefect Olybius
at Antioch, the consequence of which was that she was executed. St
Margaret's was, allegedly, one of the voices heard by Joan of Arc.

The church is based on a cruciform plan with a central tower. A
spire was added to the tower around the mid-sixteenth century, but
a new, broach spire was erected in 1760 to replace the original.
Internally the tower crossing has a vaulted roof. To the visitor
standing at the W. end of the nave, the building appears optically
much longer than it is in reality. The eye has to pass from the
relatively wide proportions of the nave, on through the narrower
tower crossing and finally into the moderately long but narrow
wagon-roofed chancel to the altar and brilliant window at the E. end.

The perspective is excellent, giving the effect of looking down a tunnel towards the light.

The church notes by John Flower of Chilmark show that there have been numerous attempts at rebuilding over the centuries. Of the present edifice probably the twelfth-century N. doorway (now resited) and two, thirteenth-century lancet windows in the N. wall at the W. end of the chancel are the earliest parts. A major reconstruction in the late thirteenth, early fourteenth-centuries saw the chancel and nave extended and the tower and transepts added. In the fourteenth century new windows were installed in the S. wall of the old portion of the nave; it was then that the S. porch was erected. The S. doorway was replaced in the fifteenth century.

Prior to entering the churchyard one has to pass through the large memorial lychgate complete with a rarely-seen coffin-stone for resting the coffin before carrying it into the church. On either side the S. doorway are two carved and worn period figures. Also there are two memorial stones, dated 1666, to two members of the Fricker family; father and son, their remains being buried in the porch.

An architect who figures very largely in this part of Wiltshire was Thomas Henry Wyatt (1807–1880). Wyatt was a designer at whom English architectural historians delight in taking an artistic and intellectual swipe, as they consider him guilty of all the excesses of Victorian church vandalism; not without reason, nor was he alone. (*See Fonthill Gifford and East Knoyle.*) In 1856 he greatly restored and extended St Margaret's, removing a western gallery and its external stairway, adding the stair turret and enlarging the N. transept and N. aisle with a four-bay arcade. Wyatt resited the twelfth-century N. doorway at the W. end of the N. aisle, marking and rebuilding the stonework almost in its original form.

There is a ring of six bells, two cast in the fifteenth century, one each from 1613 and 1616; the treble and tenor were added in 1877. The entire ring was re-tuned and re-hung in 1974. The ringing chamber is not in the tower but is situated in the crossing area forward of the nave, and the memorial bell ropes from 1984 come snaking through the vaulted crossing roof and into the crossing itself.

In the S. transept is the Chapel of the Ascension, renovated and consecrated in 1977 as part of HM the Queen's Silver Jubilee thanksgiving.

St Margaret's abounds with memorials, and other tokens of esteem and love. To these memorials are attached feelings of loss and despair, individually and collectively; one can feel this very palpably on a tour of this lovely church. It is a very moving experience, detecting the deep trauma of the donors, followed by a resolution through belief in an afterlife. To single out one memorial is both difficult and yet easy for there was one event in the parish which affected not only a family but the whole community; the profoundly tragic death by fire, in 1989, of the three young daughters of the newly appointed Vicar and his wife, Revd and Mrs Malcolm Anderson. Their memorial is in the form of new chancel lighting; sensitive and appropriate.

The WW1 memorial in the churchyard, most unusually and rarely, carries the name of a female; Annie Moores. She went to France after her brother's death where she too was killed, whilst working as a nurse.

COMPTON ABBAS
– North Dorset

On the A350 between Shaftesbury and Blandford.
O.S.Landranger 183.

Dedicated to Saint Mary

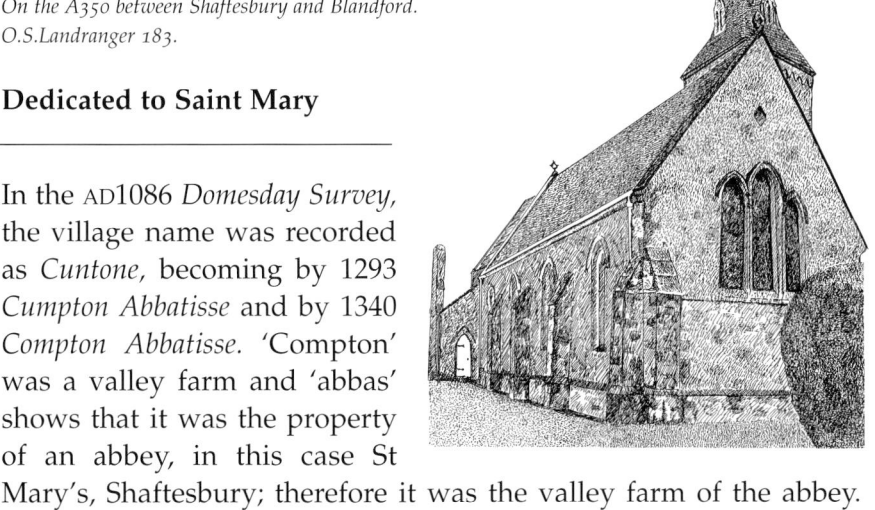

In the AD1086 *Domesday Survey*, the village name was recorded as *Cuntone*, becoming by 1293 *Cumpton Abbatisse* and by 1340 *Compton Abbatisse*. 'Compton' was a valley farm and 'abbas' shows that it was the property of an abbey, in this case St Mary's, Shaftesbury; therefore it was the valley farm of the abbey. Following the Dissolution of St Mary's in 1539, the estates which the abbey held were also affected. During the reign of Henry VIII, in September 1544, Compton Abbas manor and advowson *(see Upton Noble)* were granted to Sir Thomas Arundell, when he also purchased Melbury Abbas and the Donheads. However, a note in the church claims that the estate was held by Sir Thomas Wriothesley, Earl of Southampton, but that was probably during the reign of Edward VI.

'Having become very dilapidated, a new church has recently been built on a more convenient site at West Compton, close to the turnpike-road from Blandford to Shaftesbury.' – Hutchins. The turnpike-road is now the A350, following the same alignment as before; the church is immediately adjacent to it. The former church of St Mary, with only its west tower and part of a wall still intact, is situated about half-a-mile distant, close to East End farm at East Compton. This is the church where Thomas Bravell, one of the leaders of the Dorset Clubmen *(see Iwerne Courtney)* was Rector. Bravell was arrested in 1645 and 'sequestered', which probably meant that his freedom of movement was restricted.

The current church, designed by George Evans of Wimborne was built between 1866–7 at a total cost of £2,430 (old money), and consecrated by the Bishop of Salisbury on 11 February 1868. (Evans also designed St Andrew's, Fontmell Magna, St Thomas', Melbury Abbas and St John the Evangelist at Poxwell, near Dorchester.)

The church which Evans conceived, its stonework now attractively patinated and embossed with lichen, is small, charming and rich in some of its architectural detail; compact, but by no means plain. To see St Mary's from the S. side is to appreciate its lovely edifice which delicately graces the surrounding sylvan setting. Its S. doorway entrance is precisely carved and generous in its proportions and the stepped-buttressing, strengthening the tower, rises to just below what appear to be triple bell-openings. In fact only the central opening on each face of the tower is functional, those to left and right are imaginatively styled blind arcades. There is no embattled top stage; the broached spire rests on the edge of the tower, curving gently upwards with attractive lucarnes and gablets situated towards its lower level. The semi-circular outside stair-turret, with conical capping, fits snugly into the SW angle of the nave and tower. Near to the vestry entrance on the N. side, a further attractive external feature is an impressive and dignified high chimney-stack, designed, no doubt, to carry away the smoke from the Victorian heating system of the church.

In the tower is a ring of five bells: number 1 of 1875 is by James Bartwell of Birmingham; number 2 (1897 V.R.) [Queen Victoria's Diamond Jubilee] is inscribed, *Laus Deo*; number 3 (1616) is by John Wallis *(see Fifehead Magdalen)* and bears his initials in the inscription, *Searve God IW*; number 4 (*c.*1500) is inscribed, *Maria*; number 5 (1624) is by John Danton, bearing his initials ID in the inscription, *Remember God ID. RT.*

Internally the E. end has a polygonal apse with attractive stone rib-vaulting and finely detailed carving to the capitals, which rest on slender, plain, Purbeck marble columns and a three-light arrangement of simple lancet windows. The centre, Crucifixion, light is dated 1908. The left light is dedicated to Marie Cryer (d.1949), whilst the right is dedicated to her husband Alfred (d.1940). Both windows are of a very high artistic quality; imaginatively and skilfully executed. The Victorian floor tiles are by the Herbert Minton factory. *(See Upton*

Noble.) Whilst in the chancel, note the tiny pipe organ, in particular its size and scale. It was manufactured by the Positive Organ Company Ltd., London, and bears the serial number 695. A plate records the instrument's restoration in 1947. *(See Fifehead Magdalen.)*

Mary Buchanan's church notes of 1997 inform the visitor that in 1968 – the year of St Mary's Church centenary – a parclose screen was erected in the S. aisle, between the two arcades, creating an attractive chapel. Above the chapel altar is a stained and painted light of a quatrefoil design. In front of the altar is a small carpet into which is woven the Greek word *OIKOUMENE* – 'all the world' (Matthew 24:14). A curious and interesting furnishing in the chapel is the elegant and exotic sanctuary lamp which derived from the village of Sonai, in the Almadnagar district of Bombay where it hung in a Hindu temple before a statue of Kali. The villagers, on being converted to Christianity, allowed the SPG (Society for the Propagation of the Gospel) missionary to take it away. On returning to England she requested that the lamp should also be converted to Christian use.

The great artistic gem of St Mary's has to be the Annunciation W. window of the mid 1950s, by Francis Skeat. The background to the figures shows Compton Down and the old church tower. The window is illuminated with the most subtle colour; the figures, divine and human, are beautifully drawn and their clothing finely shaded and modelled. Francis Walter Skeat FRSA was born in 1909 in St Albans, Herts. and educated at the Whitgift School, Croydon. He began designing in 1934, for Christopher Webb, moving to London in 1936 to work for Wippell Mowbrays. From 1946–54 he was at 69, Hazelwood Drive, St Albans and from 1954 to around 1988 at The White House, 5, Cross Lane, Harpenden. The window here is probably from the latter period. Skeat later moved to Sweden. Some of his work can be seen in St Alban's Abbey, St Peter's Church, St Albans (1934), St John's, Boldre, Hants. (1956) and St George's Chapel, Lincoln Cathedral (1969). His artist's mark differs over the years: a standing hart (symbol of Hertfordshire) within a shield *c.*1935; a seated hart with his name; a standing figure of St Francis with birds and his initials FS or FWS.

The Norman font, possibly twelfth-century, is from the old church. It has a tub-shaped bowl decorated with a re-cut, raised foliate scroll pattern; the base is Victorian.

Should the church pilgrim visit the three churches at Iwerne Courtney, Sutton Waldron and Compton Abbas – all on the A350 – during a morning or afternoon they may well be in need of refreshment. Quite by chance, next to St Mary's, Compton Abbas, is the Milestones Tea Rooms, housed in a picturesque seventeenth-century cottage which was here, next to the old turnpike road, when the church was built in 1866. Rest in the quiet garden at the rear and observe again the lovely tower and spire of St Mary's, Compton Abbas.

COMPTON PAUNCEFOOT

– East Somerset

South of A303(T), west of Wincanton.
O.S.Landranger 183.

Dedicated to
Saint Mary the Virgin

Compton Pauncefoot is another poetically named English village. Compton relates to a 'valley farm', a member of the Pauncefoot family owned it, therefore, it was Pauncefoot's Manor. The farm belonged to the Pauncefoot family until 1493 and, through two daughters, it was eventually shared by the Whyting and Keynes families.

Prior to this, at the time of the *Domesday Survey* of 1086, the place was referred to as *Cuntone* and Turstin Fitzrolph held the land. Turstin is shown as the thirty-fifth largest landowner after King William (out of a total of forty-seven, holding land in Somerset). A mill was catalogued, as were fifteen acres of meadow and four furlongs of woodland in length, by one furlong broad. Of the human inhabitants, there were nine *villans* (a higher economic class of peasant), eleven *bordars* (an economically lower class of peasant); both groups shared five ploughs. The title Villan is from the Latin *villanus* – a villager. Bordar, or cottager, is from the Norman French *borde* – a hut. The Domesday scribe further recorded that there were four slaves; at the bottom, economically and socially. Therefore, *(based on the calculations illustrated for Buckhorn Weston)* the total population was probably around one-hundred and eight. The landscape around this part of East Somerset is beautiful, intensely rural and tranquil. To seriously enlarge the village here would be an appalling act of abomination against the natural environment and the existing social order.

In 1485 Sir Walter Pauncefoot left a sum of money for the building of a church and a chantry. Most of the church is, therefore, fifteenth-century Perp. period in style. The addition of a N. aisle in 1864 is the only major alteration to that first structure; nave, S. aisle, S. porch and tower. The tiny church of St Mary's which appears dignified and of noble countenance is built from Ham stone and because it is not in the least pressed for space, by no means forbidding. The W. tower has a plain parapet with a lightly ornamented spire.

Passing from the low light level of the S. porch into the nave the glow from the stained and painted glass is quite a contrast; the windows breathe fire. Every window is filled with vigorous colour; mostly pictorial but some geometric and foliate. The two pictorial windows in the N. aisle, the main E. end window in the chancel, the E. window in the Lady Chapel and one window in the S. wall of the S. aisle are by Jean-Baptiste Capronnier of Brussels (1814–91), who worked from around 1860 to 1885. His father, François (1789–1833), worked for the Sèvres porcelain factory, eventually leaving to set up his own workshop where he was joined by his son Jean-Baptiste. Capronnier is little known in England, but a number of churches, particularly in North and South Yorkshire, possess windows in his very distinctive style. He exhibited at the Great Exhibition of 1851, along with a number of continental stained glass artists including Giuseppe Bert(oll)ini *(see Tollard Royal)*, as a result of which he received many commissions. Capronnier gained an international reputation; his work also being installed in some American churches. At St Mary's his windows are from the years 1865–1877. Capronnier died in 1891 aged seventy-seven; one of his finest works can be seen in St Michaal's Cathedral, Brussels. The W. window of 1896 is by Charles Eamer Kempe. *(See Donhead St Mary.)* It has all the hallmarks of Kempe with a characteristic palette of colour; very finely drawn. This window is seen to its best advantage on a sunny evening, during the summer months.

The painted roofs of the nave and chancel are superb, particularly the ceiling panels in the chancel depicting angels bearing the instruments of the Crucifixion; hammer, nails etc. On the N. and S.

sides of the chancel are two windows in a modern style which are inspiring. The one to the N. is dedicated to the first Lord Blackford and the S. window, which shows a uniformed Royal Air Force Flight Sergeant from WWII, is dedicated to, 'Ann and William Mason and the tragedy of war.' Both windows are straightforward and of great artistic merit; a poignant reminder of the debt we owe to those who served our country in the past and an encouragement for our endeavour to hold fast to those same ideals. They were designed by Hugh Ray Easton (1906–65). His windows were crafted by Hendra and Harper of Harpendon, Herts. and Easton's artist's mark included an H H monogram, clearly visible in these two windows.

St Mary's is an uncomplicated church and its simplicity is perhaps best summed up in the inspirational words of St Paul in his letter to the Philippians:

> … *Whatsoever things are true, whatsoever things are honest, whatsoever things are just, whatsoever things are pure, whatsoever things are lovely, whatsoever things are of good report; if there be any virtue, and if there be any praise, think on these things.* **(Philippians 4:8)**

CUCKLINGTON
– East Somerset

South of the A303(T), off the B3081,
between Wincanton & Bourton.
O.S.Landranger 183.

Dedicated to
Saint Lawrence

Down a short, narrow lane, with blue and white painted cottages on the left and a high wall on the right, is the very picturesque church of St Lawrence. It is not large but, because other buildings close by are relatively small, it rears up above them in an attractive village grouping. The original builders sited the church perfectly, possessing a perceptive eye for the spirit of the location. With one's back to the W. wall the ground in front drops away very sharply and the broad panoramic view in front is just, well, magnificent; Wincanton is on the right and almost straight ahead is Cadbury, some nine miles away, and beyond.

Another attractive Somerset village church. St Lawrence's, Cucklington has a neatly finished embattled top to the tower and a string course with corner gargoyles below; simple and unaffected. On the S. wall of the tower is an inscription dated 1703 which bears the name of the rector and the churchwardens at that time. The church notes state that it was customary in the eighteenth century to commemorate restoration work in this manner. The pretty church clock above the inscription also dates from around that period. Sitting perkily on the top of the tower is a small, white painted cupola; a fine feature adding a touch of brio set against the skyline. This too probably relates to the restoration work on the tower. Let's put this into context: 1703 was the year of the national Great Storm which lasted for two days in late November, 8,000 people perished and the trail of destruction was enormous; Queen Anne had ascended the throne just one year earlier and John Churchill, Duke of Marlborough, was seeing off the French (again!) with victories at Ramillies, Oudenarde, Malplaquet and, of course, Blenheim; on the European Continent in the same year J S Bach was appointed organist at the church of St Boniface, Arnstadt – he was eighteen years old.

Internally there are some interesting architectural touches. The N. aisle arcading is probably the oldest part of the church, together with the unmistakably Norman font. Remaining on the N. side, the arch from the chancel into what was the N. transept is Late Perp. (convincing, but is it original?) This area at the rear of the organ is now the vestry. On the N. wall the marble inscription informs that below this area is the vault of the Dalton family. The wall tablets, installed in 1819, record the burial dates of the Dalton family from 1706 to 1903.

Because the church is sited on sloping ground, the chancel is situated at a higher level than the nave and then there are a further three steps up to the sanctuary. The effect is imposing. It would be a good setting for the staging of a medieval mystery play from one of the great York or Wakefield cycles; it is a ready-made theatre.

The entrance to the S. transept, the site of St Barbara's Chapel, is through a handsome arrangement of tripartite arches. This work was carried out by G R Crickmay ARIBA, of Weymouth (1830–1907), in 1880 when he made other restorations on the building. Crickmay's best church, locally, is Holy Trinity, Weymouth (1887). (Thomas Hardy worked as an architect for Crickmay at one time.) In the E. window of the chapel there is an insertion of a small gem of fifteenth-century glass, depicting the figure of St Barbara. To her right and above is a further fragment of a painted trefoil which probably relates to Richard Bere, Abbot of Glastonbury (1493–1524). Part of Bere's personal heraldic arms was a pun, or rebus, on his name; a beer barrel. Additionally, in the S. transept there are two attractive pedimented wall tablets to the Watts family dated 1716 and 1729.

Of the two saints connected with the church St Lawrence, to whom it is dedicated, died in Rome AD258 (his Feast Day is 10th August).

He was ordered by the City Prefect to hand over his church's valuables. Lawrence gathered together a number of the sick and poor and presented them to the Prefect, telling him that they were the church's treasures. As a result he, according to tradition, was put to death by being roasted on a gridiron which became his symbol. (Another version suggests he was beheaded.) On either side of the chancel arch are two carvings; one of the head of St Lawrence, the other a gridiron. The other Saint, Barbara, has no fixed death date but it ranges from AD235 to 313, and in numerous places; Egypt, Rome and elsewhere, (her Feast Day is 5th December). She was locked in a tower by her father, to hide her beauty, as a result of which, out of loneliness and desperation, she became a Christian. On refusing to renounce her new faith her father denounced her to the authorities who forced him to put her to death, himself. He carried out the execution at the top of the tower and was immediately struck by lightning and reduced to ash. There is absolutely no evidence that Barbara really existed; the story springs from a published pious romance. Nevertheless St Barbara's cult spread, on the basis that she could be invoked against lightning. Her symbol is a tower.

There has to be a reason why St Barbara has a chapel specifically dedicated to her here at Cucklington. A note in the church porch declares that the village well is dedicated to St Barbara, known in local folklore tradition by her pet name of 'Bab-Babwell', patron saint of hills.

Centuries ago churches were generally the highest buildings, particularly those with spires. Before the concept and invention of the lightning conductor it was fairly common practice to place some saintly relics in a box and site them near to the tops of spires or towers in an attempt to ward off and protect the building from a lightning strike. Considering the topographic position of Cucklington church and its relation to the landscape, perched as it is in a prominent position on the rim of that vast shallow bowl to the west of the church, the natural potential for damage just here must have loomed very large in people's minds; superstition must also have been a very powerful force. Was the reason for dedicating a chapel to St Barbara a means of invoking her protection from a powerful electrical storm and assuaging anxiety and fear?

St Lawrence's has had a number of generous benefactors over the centuries. The Phelips of Montacute were patrons of the living between 1766 and 1953. Fund raising for the express purpose of the restoration of the church in 1873 took place during the rectorship of Chandos Phelips. William Phelips was the patron at the beginning of the work and James Phelips continued after his death. The three-light E. window was a gift from the Phelips family in 1874. Around the time of Crickmay's restoration the same family also donated the beautifully rendered pulpit and reredos, both now in a superb condition of maturity; the carvings having a wonderful patina. These were crafted by a talented Belgian craftsman, M Vermeylen of Louvain, signed and dated 1890. Apart from being benefactors, one of the Phelips family, Miss C A Phelips, carved the excellent reading desk and worked on the choir stalls, based on designs provided by Crickmay in the 1880s. The organ by Flight & Robson (not now in its original position) was donated in 1818 by Nathaniel Dalton.

It is not simply the material benefits of the donations which have been made to St Lawrence's over the years which have given the building its unique qualities. There is also a strong feeling that the church is genuinely loved and well used, which is conveyed to the visitor in a manner which is most welcoming. St Lawrence's is more than just another attractive Somerset church.

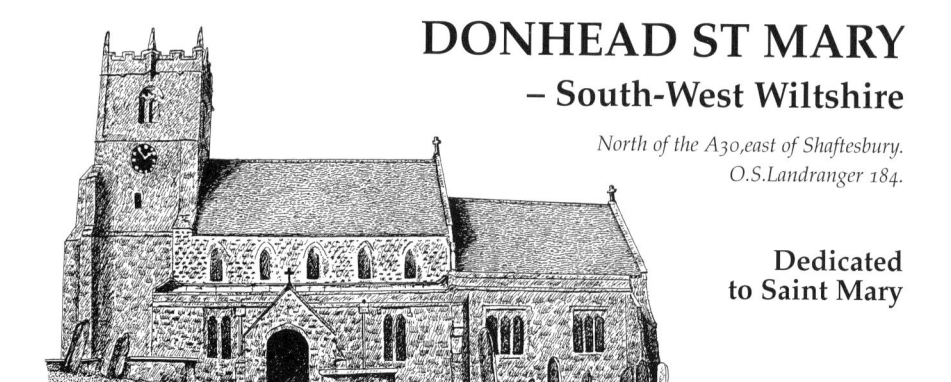

DONHEAD ST MARY
– South-West Wiltshire

North of the A30,east of Shaftesbury.
O.S.Landranger 184.

**Dedicated
to Saint Mary**

In the fervent words of the Psalmist: *How lovely is thy dwelling place, O Lord of hosts!* From the south, St Mary's presents its handsome Gothic stepped profile; from tower, to nave, to chancel in descending order. The Perp. period W. tower (although the ground stage is likely earlier) has four corner pinnacles, with additionally a central pinnacle, on corbels, between each corner of the embattled parapet. The entire building is fashioned from local greensand and the fourteenth-century S. porch, with its stone pointed tunnel-vaulted roof, is heavily and attractively buttressed. Turning around at the porch to gain the wider view from the high point here at Donhead, or Down Head, the wide and sweeping landscape looking towards the south-east descends, then rises to Win Green and part of the Cranborne Chase.

The discovery of pottery sherds reveals that St Mary's was, almost certainly, built on an AD second-century Romano-British site. Pevsner has it that there was an aisleless Norman church on the site in the twelfth century and a very small length of frieze, once below the eaves, which can be seen on the S. wall of the N. aisle, supports Pevsner's expert observation. However, later in the twelfth century aisles were added; the S. being the first.

The very high nave was given single-light clerestory windows during the thirteenth century. There are three bay arcades in the N. and S., the S. having strongly carved thirteenth-century capitals whilst the N. are plain.

The large and airy chancel, rebuilt in the fifteenth century and probably extended is both fair and eye-catching, with arcading of two bays leading to the side chapels of the Perp. period, the tracery of the fenestration being well-carved and preserved. The church has some excellent glass notably the E. window dedicated in 1882 to Richard White Blackmore, a former Rector, who died aged ninety. In the S. wall of the S. chapel is the very striking and beautiful Dunston Memorial window of 1984, which combines painted, stained and etched elements. This window, designed and made by Henry Haig, *(see Semley)* is dedicated to Frederick Warburton Dunston, his wife Louisa Camilla and their seven children; the root of the theme is *The Presentation of Christ in the Temple.* It is suggested, by a note in the church, that the windows in the N. chapel are probably by Kempe in the 1860s. *(See Longbridge Deverill and Bourton.)* The windows of the four Evangelists are particularly well drawn and delicate, the glasswork affecting the senses whilst still retaining its spirituality. The three-light W. window of the nave is dedicated to the Revd Thomas Warburton.

Charles Eamer Kempe (1834–1907) was both a prolific glass painter and designer of ecclesiastical furnishings. As a young man he devoutly wished to take Holy Orders but an unfortunately severe speech defect prevented him from following his vocation. Born in Brighton, he was brought up in a strongly convinced Tractarian household. The Tractarians were so-called after a series of pamphlets *Tracts for the Times* appeared between the years 1833 and 1841 to act as a defence of their High Church or High Anglican doctrines; a counter-blast to the decayed standards of the church in worship, ritual, the physical condition of many churches, and their deep concern with social conditions in society. The Tractarians, also known as the Oxford Movement, was started by Dr E B Pusey, professor of Hebrew at Oxford; Revd Dr John Keble and the Revd J H Newman, who wrote the first Tract (later he converted to Roman Catholicism and eventually became cardinal). The Tracts influenced ecclesiastical art and architecture for the rest of the century and beyond.

Kempe considered that if he could not conduct a ministry in the chancel and sanctuary he could, through his talents, raise their significance and status by beautifying them. He studied for a short time with the already well established company of Clayton and Bell. *(See Silton.)* On leaving that company he set up his first studio at home in London in 1869. Many of his designs show a preference for a fifteenth-century Düreresque style which he had studied whilst sketching on visits to Europe. Kempe's work became recognisable through his brilliant employment of a colour palette of gold, silver of an opalescent quality, a distinctive ivory white, strong dark greens, blue and blue-grey, and what became a major characteristic colour in his windows, a sumptuous, tawny-golden-red-brown. He often placed his single figures under an ornate architectural canopy and standing on a pedestal. The effect is like looking at a carved figure in a niche on a wall of a church. As his company grew he eventually employed from fifty to one hundred staff, engaged in stained-glass, decorative work and furnishings; it became one of the largest Victorian companies engaged in this work. On his death, in 1907, the company was taken over by a cousin Walter Ernest Tower, who had little or no experience in the company's business, as a result of which the staff were profoundly shocked at his appointment. Tower remained with the company until it finally closed in 1934; sixty-six years after it started. One of the last orders to be completed was for the church of St John the Baptist, Frome, Somerset.

In her informative and photographically illustrated, semi-biographical/historical work on Charles Eamer Kempe and his company, *Master of Glass*, Margaret Stavridi (1906–2001), whose father John William Lisle, was chief draughtsman for Kempe, explains in detail the firm's stained-glass trademarks. Kempe used three wheatsheaves on an heraldic shield background in the 1880s and a single golden wheatsheaf from 1895 as his artist's marks. Possibly Kempe used the former for personally known donors of windows or incumbents of churches. In some windows an A.E.T. monogram can be found; Alfred Edward Tombleson was Kempe's master glass painter and this device was sometimes used in the 1890s after the single wheatsheaf had been adopted. On very important works, for example in the cathedrals of Hereford, Chester and

Lichfield, Kempe used his entire coat-of-arms (to which he was entitled, of which the wheatsheaf was part), but in Winchester, his Jubilee window of 1897, he left without mark. When Walter Tower took over the company a tower symbol superimposed on a single golden wheatsheaf, was used as a signature. This mark can often be found on one light, in the left-hand corner. Owen Chadwick, in *The Victorian Church* wrote, ' … the art of stained glass reached its zenith, not with the aesthetic innovations of William Morris or Edward Burne-Jones but in the Tractarian artist Charles Eamer Kempe.'

The Jacobean period pulpit is very well crafted and the circular stone font, with an interlaced upper band and arcading, is genuine Norman of the late twelfth century. It has a wonderful aura with a strong, physical sense of time passing.

There are numerous wall tablets installed in St Mary's and one in particular, in the tower-well S. wall, is of great interest. It is dedicated to Dom Anthelm Guillemet of Bourbon in Normandy. He died in Coombe in 1798 age eighty-eight. Dom Anthelm was one of five monks who sought refuge in this, at that time, very remote area during the French Revolution.

St Mary's is a beautiful village church having a very strong peaceful ambience within this verdant, very rural and private part of south–west Wiltshire.

EAST KNOYLE – South-West Wiltshire

On the A350, Shaftesbury to Warminster road.
O.S.Landranger 183.

Dedicated to
Saint Mary
the Virgin

Lector Si Monumentum Requiris Circumspice,

(Reader, if you seek his monument, look around you.)

Thus runs the famous architect Sir Christopher Wren's epitaph in St Paul's Cathedral, London. If you seek his father Dr Christopher Wren's monument, look around you in the Chancel of St Mary the Virgin, East Knoyle.

Wren, père, was Rector here from 1623. Immediately prior to that, in 1620, he had been Rector of Fonthill Bishop; his first appointment, following St John's College, Oxford and ordination. It was in Fonthill Bishop that he met and married Mary, the daughter and heiress of local landowner Robert Cox; he was thirty-four, she twenty. Wren was a talented and scholarly man of whom his grandson, also named Christopher Wren (1675–1747), one time MP for Windsor, wrote in 1740, 'My Grandfather was a Learned Man, skillful in all the Branches of Mathematicks'. The Rector was also a trained architect, receiving a commission in 1634 to design a costly building for Queen Henrietta Maria, wife of Charles I. Wren, fils, was born here on the 20th October 1632, his birthplace not the Rectory, but a small cottage at the bottom of Wise Lane, now no longer in existence.

Dr Wren contributed, artistically, to the enhancement of the chancel in St Mary's Church in an entirely unique manner. A visit to St Mary's to see the work, if solely for that reason, is worth the effort. All the walls, and originally the ceiling, are adorned with plaster figures and texts. The W. wall above the chancel arch shows what now remains of a depiction of *Christ's Ascension to Heaven*. Dr Wren's plasterer, Robert Brockway, left a description of this particular scene, '… a picture of the twelve Apostles and Christ ascending in the cloudes, nothing seen but his feet and the lower part of His garment below the cloudes.' Nicholas Pevsner suggests that the work was carried out in 1639. The scholarly Sir Richard Colt Hoare of Stourhead House thought the entire work of plaster enrichments as, '… a strange and quaint performance,' which he refers to in his *History of Wiltshire*. The figures are certainly a strangely mystical display, very loosely akin to Stanley Spencer's paintings, however any direct similarity should not be pressed too hard. The great tragedy of Dr Wren's work is that so much of it is now no more.

The E. wall portrays Jacob's Dream with angels ascending and descending ladders (Genesis 28:10-12). The S. wall shows the Sacrifice of Isaac (Genesis 22:1-19). The N. wall shows a man kneeling, arms raised in supplication, and above him a dove along with the text of Psalm 55. Possibly it was whilst working on some of these images, suggests the excellent church guide book by Anthony Claydon of East Knoyle, that Roundhead soldiery, pursuing Royalists from Warminster, burst into the church. (The Civil War began in 1642, and Dr Wren was well known for his strong Royalist sympathies. His brother, Matthew, a bishop was imprisoned for his adherence to the Royalist cause.) Completely misreading the situation, the Parliamentarian soldiers wrong-headedly removed the Rector from his church. Dictators and their disciples throughout history, including more modern times, have shown an ignorant and intolerant suspicion of art, which comes with an illiberal caste of mind inducing anxiety and fear. Thinking these images were of a Papist nature they set to, in their iconoclastic manner, smashing the heads of the apostles in the Ascension scene. Dr Wren was allowed back into the church when the soldiers were satisfied the work related to the Ascension. However, the Rector's figures brought him into conflict with the Parliamentarians again in 1647, which then led to him being charged with heretical practices. *(See the church guide for a fuller account of the latter.)* Restoration work was attempted on the Ascension around 1850, but some of the original damage is still visible.

The figure, referred to above, kneeling in supplication could probably be Dr Wren himself, and a reading of the text of Psalm 55, may give us some insight into the state of the Rector's mind around that time. In addition there are also two words in Greek capitals, the first, APTEROS, meaning 'wingless', from *pteryx* , which relates to flying. APOTEROS has a meaning of 'further off'. The Rector had an interest in Latin puzzles, some of which he had inscribed on the capitals in the chancel. These, however, were destroyed in an attack of indiscriminate architectural Victorian enthusiasm by the architect T H Wyatt. *(See Fonthill Gifford.)* Fortunately they were copied and can be seen in a publicly accessible document at the rear of the church. (For further consideration of this subject refer to, *The Nature of Knoyle* by Anthony Claydon.) Therefore, it is possible that the use of 'wingless' and 'further off', in Greek is a cryptic reference to either himself and his immediate circumstances or, perhaps, directly relates to the fact that a dovecote in his garden had been destroyed in 1638 by someone digging for saltpetre, used in the manufacture of gunpowder. *(For further information refer to the church notes on this subject.)*

To return to the chancel; it is Norman in its bones, as Pevsner described it, and Early English in its fenestration. Early in the thirteenth century it was extended and new side windows were put in. The E. window was remodelled in the fifteenth century. The current stained-glass was dedicated in 1934 to George Wyndham of Clouds House, a nearby residence. Wyndham was Secretary of State for Ireland and, amongst other things, was both a literary figure and a soldier. The window was paid for by both Houses of Parliament and executed by Sir Ninian Comper; a further example of his fine artistry and use of colour. *(See Witham Friary.)*

The intimate N. aisle chapel has a reflective and, to some minds, an ideally gloomy religious ambience. It was formerly the Still family chapel; note particularly their kingfisher crest set in one window. They in turn were followed by the Seymour and Wyndham families, their successors at Clouds House. Whilst visiting St Mary's do see the, now somewhat decayed, Wyndham burial enclosure by Detmar Blow, in the churchyard. Detmar Blow (1867–1939) was a very gifted architect with an international reputation who frequently worked in the Arts and Crafts Movement style.

The fine and handsome Perp. W. tower has battlements, pinnacles, two niches and trefoil headed bell-openings. It was restored in 1893 by Philip Webb. It has a small W. door and a six-light clear glass window. Internally the tower has a fan-vaulted ceiling beneath the bell chamber, and a handsome wooden screen. The millennium window by Patrick Reyntiens, installed in July 2000, is a courageous, bold and exciting addition to this historically important and fascinating church. Reyntiens occasionally worked with John Piper, for example in 1955 at Oundle School, Northants. and again in 1976 in the Roman Catholic Cathedral in Liverpool. St Mary's is important, not only to local history and the intriguing Dr Christopher Wren but also for its associations with his son, the nationally important figure of Sir Christopher Wren.

FIFEHEAD MAGDALEN
– North Dorset

South of the A30, between Shaftesbury and Milborne Port. O.S.Landranger 183.

Dedicated to Saint Mary Magdalene

Fifehead Magdalen, Fifehead Saint Quintin and Fifehead Neville are all villages in Dorset; their names clearly having one thing in common. In the *Domesday Survey* they were all assessed at 'five hides' each. A hide was a unit of measurement for tax. The word derives from *hid* or *hida*, best understood as 'family land', that is, the amount of land necessary to support a free peasant and his family. There appears to have been no strict measurement of a hide which ranged from around sixty to one hundred acres. A hide of good arable land was smaller than a hide of inferior quality. The RCHM in their 1972 report, record that the parish of Fifehead Magdalen covered an area of nine hundred and seventy-three acres.

The male population of *Fifhide* at the time of the *Domesday Survey* of 1086 was fourteen. Taking the average size of a family as four and a half, that makes a population of around sixty-three in total. *(See Buckhorn Weston.)* The population in 1801 was two hundred and forty but has greatly reduced since that date to about half the number. The parish registers dating from *c.*1850, when the population was two hundred and eight, are still in current use and reflect the small number of services of births, marriages and deaths in the village since then.

'It is a well inclosed parish, upon the western banks of the Stour, between the river and the parish of Stalbridge. The village is beautifully situated upon the summit of a hill, which rises with gradual ascent from the banks of the Stour.' – Hutchins.

The village is still beautifully situated, and should the visitor wish to confirm that, then look out over the wide panorama from the east end of the church. The church of St Mary Magdalene is perfect. It is a paradigm of an English village church; slightly elevated, very small, ancient and fetching, set in a tree-burdened churchyard with leaning, lichen-covered, fading and eroding tombstones.

The beauty and charm of St Mary Magdalene lies in its simplicity of form. The whole is comprised of nave, chancel, low S. tower with a renewed embattled parapet and tiny stair-turret tucked in the SW angle. This fourteenth-century building is of squared and coarse rubble with ashlar facings and stone-slated roof. On the N. side is a chapel, more properly a mortuary chapel, built *c*.1750 to the same scale as the rest of the building. The entire church underwent restoration in 1870 and 1904–5 and is still in excellent condition.

The studded, heavy oak, outer church door is of the late seventeenth century. In the S. porch, to the left, is the access door to the ringing chamber; opposite is an arched niche set into the wall, which before the Reformation was used to hold the holy water stoop. The inner door into the nave is a lovely and rare example of a centrally-divided, oak, folding door. It is wonderfully antique with a patina of centuries of use ingrained into it. A date of 1637 is carved into the right-hand panel, whilst on both panels, on either side of the central divide are 'official', non-graffito initials, also carved into the woodwork (the churchwardens?). On stepping into the tiny nave one can perhaps sense a powerful feeling of great antiquity clinging to the fabric and the warm and comfortable presence of worshippers of earlier centuries can be strongly detected in the heavy silence.

Some of the first furnishings the visitor will see are the four large, ornate, brass, globular pendant chandeliers, complete with candles in the two tiers of sconces. This very elegant form of illumination, perfect in this setting, was installed in the seventeenth century and, according to Peter Oxlade's informative notes, they are now used once a year to provide an evocative candle-lit setting for the Christmas service of nine lessons and carols.

By 1973 the plain glass in the windows was badly deteriorating and was replaced by 'reamy' glass as part of a memorial gift by Mrs N G Richards of the Manor of Fifehead. The W. window was also redesigned in the same year to act as a memorial to her husband Lieutenant-Colonel N G Richards and was part of Mrs Mary Richards' gift to the church. This stained and painted window is the work of Alan Christopher Wyrill Younger (1933–2004). Younger was educated at Alleyn's School, Dulwich and in 1954 studied at the Central School, London, where he specialised in stained-glass. Later he taught at the Royal College of Art and set up his own studio in 1966. His artist's marks have differed over the years but are always variations of the monogram AY, usually with a date attached. Younger's work can also be seen in the Great Rose window, St Alban's Cathedral (1987), the Galilee Chapel, Durham Cathedral (1972), Chester Cathedral (1992), Southwark Cathedral (1993) and the Henry VII Chapel, Westminster Abbey (2000). Sadly, Alan Younger died on 12 May 2004, whilst this book was being prepared. He has been described as, '… one of the most important stained glass artists of the post-war era, …' (obit. *Daily Telegraph* 8 June 2004).

During the restoration of 1904–5 the stonework surrounding some of the windows was re-chiselled to the design of the architect. The Good Shepherd window in the nave and the W. window in the chapel are exceptions.

The woodwork in the chancel, the church notes inform, is largely from 1904. The three-panelled painted reredos behind the altar is a well executed piece of fine art with well-controlled brushwork and excellent grouping of the figures. It depicts three events of singular importance in the life of Mary Magdalene: the left panel shows Mary sensually drying Christ's feet with her hair; the centre is a crucifixion tableaux whilst, on the right, the scene is of Mary at the sepulchre. The artist was Percy Buckman who also designed the Good Shepherd window. Percy Buckman was born in Dorset, possibly at or near Lytchett Minster, in 1865. He studied at the Royal Academy Schools and lived for some time in London.

The tiny chamber organ (known as a Casson's Patent Organ), installed here in 1904, is beautiful. It was made by the Positive Organ Co.Ltd., London. *(See Compton Abbas.)* A plate records its restoration in 1982. The Positive Organ Company was founded in 1897 by

Thomas Casson (1842–1910), the father of Sir Lewis Casson the actor (b.1875), who married the actress Dame Sybil Thorndike.

In the tower is a ring of three bells. The oldest of the trio, the tenor, inscribed *Ave Maria*, is from the fourteenth century and was cast in Salisbury; number 3, inscribed *Anno Domini 1683, EG TM CW TP* is by Thomas Purdue of Cullompton. Purdues of Somerset began bell-casting in 1584 and ceased in 1697. Number 2, the treble, is by the popular local bell founder John Wallis and bears the inscription *Prayse God IW 1595*. The John Wallis foundry cast bells in Salisbury from 1580 to 1624. Little is known of him but he had a great liking for certain phrases which he recorded on his work: *Praise God; Love God; In the Lord do I trust; God be our guide; Hope Well* and *Serve God*, are some examples, all of which were followed by his initials *IW* (Iohannes Wallis). The earliest bell by Wallis which, it is believed, is still in use is the number 2 bell at Buckland Newton, Dorset, dated 1581. He is credited as being the founder of the earliest ring of eight bells for a parish church in England, which were cast in 1602 for Bishops Canning, Wiltshire; some are still in use.

There are many memorial tablets placed throughout the church; one on the N. wall of the nave is to members of the Davidge family (established in Fifehead before 1550). The inscription on the eighteenth-century memorial is now badly eroded and those interested in the full text should consult Hutchins. There are also tablets to members of the Peacock family, including Revd Edward Peacock MA, Trinity College, Cambridge, who was vicar here for thirty years and died in 1848 aged sixty-one.

The one major outstanding memorial is in the Newman family mortuary chapel, on the N. side of the chancel. It is outstanding due to its overall size and the quality of its refined carving.

The Newman family came originally from Somerset: Cadbury, Evercreech, Charlton Musgrove, Queen Camel and Wincanton are all places which figure in their pedigree. Their blazon, Hutchins (Vol.IV) was recorded at the Herald's Visitation of Somerset in 1623 as, 'Arms: Quarterly sable and argent, 1st and 4th, three mullets of the second.'

The Newman memorial is a brilliant example of the exuberant works of art to be discovered in so many churches, particularly those in rural areas. It is on the N. wall of the chapel and can be dated to *c*.1750. The back plate, which is approximately obelisk shaped, is of black marble, the rest is made up of white, pink, grey and yellow marble. On the pediment are three portrait busts carved in white marble. At the apex of the trio, beneath an ornate cartouche, is Sir Richard Newman; below, left is his wife Frances and on the right their son, Sir Samwell. Below, set onto a rectangular panel, are three carved high-relief portraits of their daughters, each within its own medallion. The rectangular background panel has some very fine carving of wreaths and scrollwork with an intricate foliated display beneath the whole. Below the base of the memorial is the following inscription:

In memory
of Sir Richard Newman, bart. who died Dec.30, 1721.
Also of Dame Frances his wife, who died Dec.4, 1730.
Also of Sir Samwell Newman their son,
who died June 4, 1747.
And of Frances and Barbara Newman, and
Elizabeth Kitchen,
three of their daughters, who died,
viz. Frances, on the 27th day of August, 1775;
Barbara, on the 6th day of January, 1763;
and Elizabeth, on the 26th day of May, 1774.
Sir Richard and his lady had three other children,
viz. Richard, Grace, and Edmonds;
all of whom died young.

Should the visitor not generally be a churchyard explorer, then please make St Mary Magdalene, Fifehead Magdalen an exception armed with Peter Oxlade's church notes as guide. If the weather is warm and sunny you may find yourself delaying your departure for just five more minutes; that would be perfectly understandable.

FONTHILL GIFFORD
– South-West Wiltshire

Off the B3089, south-west of Hindon.
O.S.Landranger 184.

Dedicated to the Holy Trinity

Should you be a Victorian church
enthusiast or, given this specific
church, a High Victorian period
aficionado, you will be in your
architectural element. If you are
neither, please make a visit
anyway; it is well worth making
the effort. Its like cannot be seen
in any nearby village.

Holy Trinity has few English village church characteristics. It is not
even orientated on the conventional east-west axis, but faces north-
east as did the earlier edifice on this site. The reason for the departure
from the established norm was possibly that the building was
intended to impress passers-by on the nearby main road. Fonthill
Gifford is in a very rural area and, given the passage of time, the now
massive cypress trees flanking the pathway mean that the church, in
spite of its size, is almost obliterated from view from the roadway.

The visitor will either love it or loathe it. In general terms, the
church's style of architecture can be observed in countless High
Victorian public buildings in large cities and particularly the north of
England. The style captured the zeitgeist, that spirit of the age which
embodied enormous state or civic pride and confidence found in
imposing city and town halls, tricked out in all their aldermanic
splendour. When placed in parallel, the twin spheres of state and
ecclesiastical influence broadcast to the world the message that
church and state shared the same lifeblood. The British Empire had
almost reached its apogee and exemplified the acme of world power
under a Queen Empress. Victorian values are made visually manifest

45

in this particular paradigm. As John Ruskin, the Victorian writer, critic and artist, wrote: 'All good architecture is the expression of national life and character; and it is produced by a prevalent and eager national taste or desire for beauty.' Taking all the foregoing into consideration, and within its own terms of reference, it surely has to be said that Holy Trinity, Fonthill Gifford is magnificent. One might also detect in a secular sense and that in the name 'Trinity' there is an embodiment of church, state and people in unity.

The earliest recorded Rector was Nicholas Murdak in 1299. However, his church did not occupy this site. According to the brief, unaccredited but informative church notes, it lay some distance away to the north. Alderman William Beckford, one time Lord Mayor of London, bought Fonthill in 1740, created a large park, demolished the old church and erected a new one, on the same site as the existing church. Beckford's building was in the Greek or Roman style, complete with a classical columned and porticoed front. Twenty-five or so years later, it was in such a bad state that the parishioners requested their new landlord, the Marquess of Westminster to effect repairs to their church. The Marquess declined, but offered instead to erect a new one.

Thomas Henry Wyatt (1807–80), one time Diocesan Architect of Salisbury, one time District Surveyor of Hackney, designer of London's Adelphi Theatre, was commissioned to design Holy Trinity in 1866. Wyatt has been greatly criticised for his designs and for his over-restoration of churches by, for example, inappropriate grafting of heavy Victorian Gothic ideas on to more sensitive established styles. He was distantly related to a number of other architectural Wyatts, and entered into partnership with David Brandon (1813–97). Their joint masterpiece, which probably owes more to Brandon than Wyatt, is St Mary and St Nicholas' Church in Wilton (1841–5). Its design, in the Italian Romanesque style was described by John Betjeman as: 'Lombardy in Wiltshire.'

Holy Trinity has an octagonal spired tower, embellished with lucarnes and gablets, situated on the S. side of the church. The bell-stage stair-turret is in the angle of the chancel and the tower, formulated in the manner of a French chateau or Scottish baronial, as in Glamis or Inverary. Its exaggerated style in this context is imposing and elegant, with each strong buttress supporting the apsidal E. end carrying an obelisk as a final flourish. There is much emphasis of detailed exterior decoration; the extrados of the door archways are richly crocketed, and the doorways themselves are wide and high, offering a dignified entrance to the visitor .

Internally it has a wide aisleless nave, with rich and deeply carved corbels supporting the roof timbers; N. and S. transepts and an apsidal chancel. The rib vaulting in the sanctuary is in the French Gothic manner; the embellished foliate bosses add to that effect. The dim numinous light in the sanctuary and chancel brings to mind a recollection of two lines from Milton's *Il Ponseroso:*

> *Storied windows richly dight,*
> *Casting a dim religious light.*

There is a repeated use of marble in the principle column shafts and colonettes, whilst in the S. transept, the stone font is supported by alabaster shafts on a carved base. Then there is the quite breathtaking pulpit; semi-circular in shape and fashioned from contrasting coloured alabaster. It is ornamented with the heads of the four evangelists carved in deep relief, each head set upon its own medallion. Overall one's mind becomes a little overpowered; on the one hand there is a feeling of some luxuriance or sumptuousness, whilst on the other there is a lack of emotional feeling, due to its aloof cerebral detachment. However, the visual effect will long endure in the mind.

A report by the Council for the Care of Churches, in August 1987, stated: 'Fonthill Gifford is a remarkably complete example of an estate church of the High Victorian period, with all its furnishings, and one of Wyatt's best churches ...'. For whatever reason, this church is one which is powerfully memorable.

GILLINGHAM – North Dorset

On the B3092, north-west of Shaftesbury.
O.S.Landranger 183.

Dedicated to Saint Mary the Virgin

Anyone seeking visible material remains linking modern Gillingham and the surrounding area with the distant past will find them, literally, thin on the ground. Ignoring completely the material remains of pre-history, archaeology has uncovered evidence of Romano-British occupation with a small number of finds of mostly domestic artefacts from the Commonmead area of Gillingham: one large fragmented, incomplete coarseware pot and pottery shards including some Samian ware. From the wider area of Todber, three coins, Samian and coarseware pottery fragments, one largely complete pot of AD first century and the skeletal remains of a male c.AD200, on display in the town's museum, together with the Gillingham artefacts.

Saxon occupation is evidenced by a finely ornamented but broken Christian cross shaft c.AD eighth/ninth century, now permanently and appropriately in situ in the parish church. It is from this period that the name of the town emerges through an eponymous leader named 'Gylla' whose name became associated with the Saxon village or *ham*. Or does it? There is a further possible interpretation of the name; 'Gylla' was possibly a diminutive or pet name for 'Gylda'. It could derive from Old English *gyll* or Middle High German *gülle* (pool). Anton Fägersten in, *Place Names of Dorset*, suggests, ' … the *ham* of the people living near the pool district.' The first reference to Gillingham is in the *Anglo-Saxon Chronicles* and relates to a battle being fought near *Gelingaham*, in 1016, between Edmund Ironside and the Danish King Cnut at Pen. *(See Pen Selwood.)* The main focus of the encounter was clearly at Pen but, due to the movement and counter-movement of battle, the conflict bulged out in the direction of Gillingham where there was probably further contact between the two sides. Slaughtergate is cited locally as the place where the skirmish occurred.

A further mention of the town comes in 1041 when William of Malmesbury (*see Bruton*), records that a Council, or *Witangemote*, was held in Gillingham where Edward the Confessor (1003–1066) was chosen to be King in 1043. Modern scholars of this period accept that London, not Gillingham, was the place where the Council took place. One might suspect that the early chronicler, Malmesbury was, on occasions, using anecdotal evidence.

The scribes of the *Domesday Survey* conducted in 1086 record Gylla's foundation as *Gelingeham, Gelingham* and *Ingelingham*. The variations probably reflect the speech pattern and phonetic emphases of the person to whom the Commissioner or scribe was speaking. The survey also records Milton-on-Stour and Wyndham's Farm. Possibly the settlements of Madjeston, Thorngrove, Wyke and others, relate to the Domesday entries for Gillingham.

As was customary, the land was not held entirely by King William who was, nevertheless, always the premier landowner in every county. Distribution of land in this area went to: St Mary's Abbey, Cranborne (tenth after the King); St Mary's Abbey, Shaftesbury (eighteenth); Turstin Fitzrolph (thirty-second); Edwin, Godwin, Wulfwine and Edward the Huntsman, as King's Thegns; and finally Hugh FitzBaldric, whose main holding locally was in Wiltshire but who was also allocated a portion of land in Gillingham.

By the time of King Edward the Confessor, Gillingham was a Royal Manor. Hutchins quite definitely states that there was a palace built by Saxon or Norman kings for residence when they came here to hunt in the extensive and densely-forested area around Gillingham. He describes it as being half a mile east from the church on the road between Gillingham and Shaftesbury near two small rivers. It was encompassed by a moat, 9 feet deep by 20 feet broad; the entire area on which the lodge stood being 320 feet by 240 feet. The early hunting lodge later became known as King's Court Palace.

King William 'Rufus' (1056/60–1100) the third son of the Conqueror, met the Archbishop of Canterbury, Anselm, here in 1094. Rufus was constantly at odds with Anselm regarding the Archbishop's attempts to reform the Church. So verbally violent was the King and so strained the relationship, it caused Anselm to leave England. A Latin text in Hutchins, shows that Anselm was summoned by William to the country house (hunting lodge) between Shaftesbury and Gillingham to have a conversation on a certain point. The summons could, conjecturally, have been related to William's opposition to Anselm's reforms. The Church, who both made and kept the records, clearly disapproved of William. It was said, for example, that he helped himself to the churches' revenues and that he used oaths in every sentence. William of Malmesbury wrote – one might suspect censoriously and possibly somewhat mischievously – of William's debauched life with his co-evals at court who, ' … rival women in delicacy of person, to mince their gait, to walk with loose gestures and half-naked.' He appears a deeply unpopular king due, largely, to his attitude to, and treatment of, Anselm; it has been suggested that his death, supposedly the result of a hunting accident involving an errant arrow, was really an assassination. The *Anglo-Saxon Chronicles* confirms that William was, ' … to nearly all his people hateful and abominable to God … without repentance or any amendment for his deeds, he died.'

It would appear that King John (1167–1216) was a frequent visitor to King's Court Palace which he either repaired or rebuilt. An itinerary shows that between 1204–1214 he often visited Gillingham, sometimes several times during the same year.

The Palace was extended again in 1252, during the reign of Henry III (1207–1272) and a perimeter wall added to a specifically stated head-height. Reference is also made to the King's Chapel which was to have a number of refinements including stained glass showing the images of St Mary the Virgin, St Edward – King and Confessor – and St Eustace. The Queen's Chapel was also singled out for renovation.

After Edward I (1239–1307) made two visits, late 1277 and early 1278, the palace ceased to attract the kings of England and the fabric started to decay. In King John's reign there were ten royal residences in Dorset alone and nationally the number remained high until around 1272, which corresponds with the death of Henry III. Over the next two hundred and fifty years the number of royal residences dropped dramatically. This period saw the beginnings of a movement towards centralisation focussed on London. Nevertheless, it is worth noting that repairs were periodically carried out on King's Court Palace until 1354. In 1369 Edward III (1312–77) ordered that the palace be demolished. A pipe roll records that during the reign of Henry IV (1366–1413) the stone from the palace was to be carried away for erecting or repairing one of the lodges (Mardele Lodge) in the forest. Hutchins, always meticulous in his references and sources, gives the names of the contractors and costs for carrying out the work. The foundations were removed in the eighteenth century and used in the repairing of the Gillingham to Shaftesbury road.

Now, all that remains of what was obviously an extensive and important building can be seen through a series of mounds, aerial photographs offer the best view (see *King's Court – Gillingham* by Bill Shreeves), which lie beneath the turf and relate to the palace's moats and banks. These can be seen at the end of King's Court Road, off the main road to Motcombe and Shaftesbury.

For over two hundred years Gillingham was one of the main centres of royal patronage in England. The patronage and presence of kings, clerics and courtiers probably provided the area with a fair economic base. From that, one can reasonably conjecture, would stem more stable and continuing employment for some, and an increase in the standard of living for a larger number. It was also the last time when kings would be so personally and intimately connected with the expanding but, undoubtedly, very status-conscious, small town of Gillingham.

The growth of Gillingham in recent years has seen a proliferation of styles, in its domestic architecture in particular. Some townspeople question the style and quality of the new buildings whilst others welcome and enjoy the changes. The population of Gillingham in 2004 stood at around 10,000. What did the townspeople think about architectural changes in 1801 when the population stood at 2,510 or in 1838 when it was 3,000, or more particularly in 1901 when the population had risen to 4,096? There are still a few interesting buildings remaining in the town centre, largely given over to commercial usage, and these are to be found in the area west of the High Street, The Square and Queen Street, slightly to the north. These buildings provide an architectural counterpoint and most decidedly point up that which is now lost. *Around Gillingham in Old Photographs*, a collection of images edited by Peter Crocker in 1992, distinctly reveals that quality buildings existed in other areas of the town; Edwardian, Victorian and earlier. Unfortunately, a fire in 1694 destroyed forty houses plus barns and stables; another in 1742 six houses and the latest in 1981, the town centre mills.

The one singular building (or at least part of it) with a distinct claim to an antiquity of almost seven-hundred years of continuous existence and use is the parish church of St Mary the Virgin, situated in the most attractive part of the old town and standing in a well kept churchyard with pretty cottages clinging closely to it on its north and west sides. St Mary's, as the parish church, is the bridge uniting a Gillingham which is long past, with the present.

A Saxon church of some status, dedicated to St Mary, was well established in Gillingham before William's commissioners arrived to conduct their survey of the area. William subsequently gave the church of St Mary, Gillingham and its appurtenances to St Mary's Abbey, Shaftesbury, in lieu of which he gave St Mary's, Gillingham an area of land at Kingston – the site of Corfe Castle. The parish of St Mary's, Gillingham became one of the largest parishes in the County of Dorset and Hutchins gives its dimensions as forty-one miles in circumference and over fifteen thousand acres in area. However, by the 1970s it was only just over half this size in area.

The chancel and part of the N. chapel are of early-fourteenth-century origin, with major rebuilding of the rest of the church in 1838. Therefore, the building of St Mary's in the medieval period shows sufficient confidence to demolish the old Saxon building, or a large portion of it, by having the financial security to fund the new. The best dating evidence for the rebuilding is the medieval chancel itself which is in the Decorated style, that is, the second period of development of Gothic architecture which began around 1270 and lasted until around 1350. The Dec. period curvilinear tracery in the windows is quite distinct and its form found favour from around 1315 to the end of the Dec. period. The Royal Commission on Historical Monuments (RCHM) states that the E. window of the chancel, with curvilinear tracery, is of 1838. Even allowing for the possibility that the windows were replaced in 1838, a detailed drawing of St Mary's from the SE made by John Buckler in 1829, now in the British Library, shows the chancel windows in exactly the same style as the ones currently in situ. (There are also original Dec. period windows in the parish hall [formerly a schoolroom] opposite the E. end of the church, on Queen Street, removed from the old church and placed here in 1838.) Above the windows on the S. and N. side of the chancel is a carved string-course with original grotesque faces and ball-flower ornamentation, a common feature of fourteenth-century architecture. The years 1318 and 1331 had to be very significant for St Mary's. In 1318, William Clyve de Motcombe was appointed the first vicar and in 1331 a chantry chapel to St Catherine was established. These events probably figure importantly in relation to the physical building of the church. Therefore, it is cautiously suggested that St Mary's was built sometime between 1320 and 1330; that is, during the reigns of the Plantagenets; Edward II (reigned 1307–1327) and Edward III (reigned 1327–1377), the demolisher of King's Court Palace.

The general national background to the fourteenth century was one of great uncertainty, when war was constant at home and overseas. There was also the terrifying prospect of the Black Death plague (from 1348 and at intervals until 1375) which affected so many families. The population of England in 1340 numbered around two and a half to four million; this figure was reduced by about one third due to the plague when approximately one thousand villages disappeared. As a result of this major turbulence, people were driven to greater personal spiritual devotion. However, it was also a period of vitality and ambition; the wealth of the church was vast and the power of the bishops increasing.

In 1838 the W. tower of St Mary's was moved further west by twenty feet from its earlier position; part of a general enlargement of the nave. It was then heightened and the upper stage remodelled in 1908 by Charles E Ponting, the Diocesan Architect of Salisbury. The section from the string-course above the clock is the most architecturally interesting and visually exciting part of the tower with a neat, well-executed battlemented top, crocketed corner-pinnacles, crocketted string-course, gargoyles and attractive west-country tracery in the bell-openings. The W. doorway was also remodelled in 1908. On the N. side of the tower is the angular external stair-turret with internal access to the clock and bell-stages.

The oldest of its eight bells, number 4, is of 1607 (recast 1909) with the apt inscription *VOCE MEA AD DOMINUM* – ('I call to the Lord' or, put more subtly, 'My being calls to the Lord'). Bell numbers 1 and 2 are by Mears and Stainbank, London (1898); numbers 3 (1726), 6 (1721) and 8 (1726) by William Cockey of Frome, whose bells are to be found in many local churches in this area; number 5 is by Thomas and James Bilbie of Chewstoke, Somerset, (*c.*1795), who were bell-founders from 1698–1814 and number 7 (1826) is by J Kingston, Bridgewater. However, to listen to the solo voice of the separate Sanctus bell inscribed *GABREEL* quickens the spirit. *GABREEL* has proclaimed his message to Gillingham down the centuries, possibly from the beginning of the medieval church in the fourteenth century.

An undated letter, probably late-1837, from the Vicar Henry Deane to the Incorporated Church Building Society which replied in January 1838, provides a small wealth of information. In it the vicar outlines his concerns, just before the major rebuilding programme began, asking what form the alterations would take and seeking financial assistance. He describes the then contemporary nave as being fifty-three feet long by twelve feet wide, the tower stood seventeen feet, six inches into the nave and the Saxon or Norman arches, separating nave from aisles, as eleven feet, six inches high; so low that they cut off the aisles from the nave. The height of the arches, standing at eleven feet, six inches, is particularly interesting indicating that they were more likely to be Norman; whatever period, they were destroyed in 1838. In the opinion of the RCHM writing in 1972, the rebuilding of St Mary's in 1838 was the first attempt at Gothic revival style of church architecture in North Dorset.

The above quoted letter from Henry Deane additionally records the need for the rebuilding of the church. There were many large private pews belonging to Gillingham's more prominent families and the vicar wanted more free and low-rent pews for his increasing congregation. The new church was opened on 5 December 1839 at a service led by the Bishop of Salisbury, when over fifty clergy attended and the church was filled to capacity.

The architect was William Walker of Shaftesbury, who also designed St Rumbold's, Shaftesbury. His plans of St Mary's, for which he was only paid – much to his annoyance – £7, fulfilled all the requirements, including clerestory windows in the nave, but it is unfortunately lacking in imagination and style; Pevsner writing in the 1970s described it as 'indifferent'.

At the E. end of the N. aisle, where St Catherine's chapel is now situated, a chantry chapel, dedicated in 1331, existed until the Reformation when Edward VI abolished all chantry chapels. The chapel was served by its own independent priest who said prayers and masses for the souls of deceased benefactors of the chapel. (The current chapel was largely rebuilt in 1838 but there are a few residual remains from the medieval building.) By the middle of the fourteenth century the foundation of new churches had fallen quite considerably, but an individual's surplus wealth could fund a chantry. Why were chantries founded? It was thought that great spiritual benefit could be gained by the frequent offering of a mass for the dead. To achieve this a deceased person would have made provision in a legal will to the effect that a specified number of masses were to be said for them, the total cost having been agreed with the chantry priest. The poor could obviously afford only a few, usually immediately following their death. The more wealthy provided funds for a limited period, or masses to be said on anniversaries; whilst for the extremely wealthy they were to be said in perpetuity. Cardinal Beaufort, for example, requested ten thousand. A further stipulation in wills was that masses should begin immediately following death; the reason for this was the desire to be liberated from purgatory as quickly as possible. Chantry priests, usually being free of pastoral duties, had time after their offices were finished to undertake the education of local children, often in the church. This extra payment would help to supplement their incomes, poorly paid as they often were, and probably provided a pension for a retired cleric.

However, the chantry priest in Gillingham appears to have been particularly well provided for. Hutchins refers to a chantry roll relating to the chapel here. The roll was likely to have been a document now probably in the PRO, dated 1548, which recorded chantries in the reign of King Edward VI, under whom the chantries were abolished. The said document refers back to the foundation to the chantry in St Mary's. According to Hutchins the chantry was styled, 'The perpetual chantry at the altar of St Katherine the Virgin in the church of Gillingham,' during the reign of Edward III 1331. A licence, '… not to the King's detriment' (meaning that the King was not to be in any way affected, financially or otherwise, by issuing the licence) was granted to John de Sandhull to give, '… one messuage [originally – a portion of land for a dwelling house] and fifty-eight acres of land and pasturage for six oxen and one heifer in Gillingham and Milton to a chaplain to celebrate divine service in the church of St Mary de Gillingham, every day forever.' John de Sandhull was probably the person who wished to endow the chantry and, even though the land referred to was his, he would still have to petition the King, who in theory owned all the land in England, to obtain permission. When the chantry was dissolved under Edward VI it was worth six pounds, fourteen shillings and four pence. It seems possible that teaching may have taken place here because the governors of Sherborne School decided to petition, which they did successfully, that the lands in Gillingham, Milton, Cumber Mead and Silton belonging to the chantry of St Katherine should be granted to them. Most certainly, in this case, it is revealed that the income from chantries was used either to found grammar schools or to assist those already in existence. According to the registers in the Salisbury Diocesan Archive in Trowbridge, twenty-one priests served St Katherine's chantry between 1333 and 1541. The last was Galfryd

Gyll, who at its dissolution in 1553 retired with a pension of five pounds per annum. Some of St Mary's finest memorials, in a church which abounds in them, are in this chapel.

The Jesop Memorial, now forlornly sited behind the organ, is dedicated to Dr John Jesop and his brother Dr Thomas Jesop. Effigies of the two brothers lie side by side on a tomb-chest under a hemispherical arch. The entire memorial, now deteriorating badly, is a finely executed and well-proportioned work which shows, in the upper section, the family arms, a figure of 'Time', with a scythe (now missing) and two reclining, sorrowing angels. Unfortunately the inscriptive panel has gone. (See Hutchins for full text.) The two life-size figures are attired in academic gowns complete with ruffs. Both brothers were graduates of Oxford University; Thomas (d.1615) was a scholar of Merton College (Collegi Mertoniensis), a Justice of the Peace for Dorset and a physician in Gillingham. John (d.1625) was educated at All Souls College (Collegi Omnium Animarum) and graduated with a degree in Divinity and was elected to a Fellowship. He was vicar of St Mary's and Prebend of Salisbury Cathedral.

The memorial to Frances Dirdoe of Milton-on-Stour is both poignant and memorable. She was the youngest of fifteen children, and the first to die, aged thirty-four, from a lingering disease, so the inscription informs us, on 18 January 1733. The white-veined marble memorial, 18 feet high, is in the form of a classical facade with an upper pediment; the Dirdoe arms above the apex. A central panel carved in deep relief shows three figures posed and draped as the Three Graces and represents Frances with her sisters Rebecca and Rachael as supporters; they were, in fact, executrixes of her estate. A memorial to Sir Henry Dirdoe, the father of Frances, is in the sanctuary area of the chancel.

All the stained and painted glass in St Mary's is Victorian, except the window above the entrance to the Chapel of the Good Shepherd. Unfortunately none of the high quality Victorian work is either signed or shows makers' marks. The theme of the E. window is the Life of Jesus. The style and colour intensity of this window suggest that it may be by John Hardman & Co. *(See Sturminster Newton.)*

Alas, about one quarter of the window is lost to view owing to the height of the memorial reredos in front. It is in memory of Capt Walter and Lieut Philip Matthews who were killed in WWI; donated by Mrs Matthews and (by 1926 the date it was dedicated) her late husband, G G Matthews, to whom it is also dedicated.

The reredos is an intricate and finely executed work of sculpture carved in deep relief, from Nailsworth stone. The subject is the *Adoration of the Infant Saviour*; the artistically grouped figures range from the infant and his mother seated under a canopy at the centre of the tableau, fading to the less prominent figures in the middle-distance, receding further to the figures, in low relief, at the rear. It is a sensitive, dignified and elegant concept both in design and execution. It was designed by H B Burke Downing ARIBA, of London (1865–1947) and carved by the internationally renowned sculptor Nathaniel Hitch when he was eighty. The quality of his work is of the very highest and can be seen in Westminster Abbey, Truro Cathedral, Washington, Sydney, Adelaide and Calcutta Cathedrals and Budleigh Salterton church, Devon. Hitch died in 1938 aged ninety-two and, according to A F H V Wagner, he was still working well into his eighties. Also in the chancel, below the S. windows, is the fourteenth-century piscina and the remains of a sedilia of the same date, but with restorations.

Gillingham can be justifiably proud of keeping faith with, and holding dear, the memory of those many who through duty and service gave their lives in the past two world wars. In keeping with that spirit, the Chapel of the Good Shepherd is undeniably the most beautiful and spiritual part of the church. This intimate chapel, at the E. end of the S. aisle, was given as a memorial by Mr and Mrs Carlton Cross of Wyke Hall in memory of their son Lieut Reginald Carlton Cross aged twenty-six, killed in France on 7 June, 1918, and whose original wooden gravemarker is in the chapel. Lieut Cross is buried in the British Cemetery at Covin near Arras. W D Caröe was the architect for the chapel, dedicated in January 1922 by the Bishop of Salisbury. Above the entrance to the chapel is the most modern stained-glass in the church dedicated to Bishop Robert Abbott, one time vicar of Gillingham. The window was designed by Powell and Sons in 1929 and the theme shows events in Bishop Abbott's ministry. Powell and Sons was a large company employing, at various times, Edward Burne-Jones and Henry Holiday (*see Mere*) as chief designers. Entrance to the chapel is enabled by descending a small flight of steps, a device which gives the space its intimate ambience. Caröe's design was to avoid the obscuring of light from the S. windows. There is some very fine quality carving particularly in the reredos and the oaken canopy above. The reredos depicts three figures: in the centre is Christus Consolator, on the right St George of England and on the left St Louis of France. The text above is from the Nicene Creed, *Qui propter nos homines* (Who for us men). On the SW wall of the chapel is a tablet to the memory of Mrs Emily Cross who died in 1927 and on the N. wall is the dedicatory inscription for the chapel, 'A.M.D.G. (*Ad Maiorem De Gloriam* – To the Greater Glory of God) To the glory of God this chapel is given by Carlton and Emily Cross of Wyke Hall, in this parish, in proud and unfading memory of their dearly loved son, Reginald Carlton Cross Lieut Dorset Yeomanry …'

Due to the donations of large numbers of wall-tablets, memorials, stained-glass, furnishings, a fine-art reredos and a chapel, the overriding impression is that for centuries the people of Gillingham have been devoted to their parish church and the large part which it so clearly played in their lives and the lives of those who are remembered so dearly.

This record has to be highly selective but for those wishing a fuller understanding of Gillingham's history, it would be useful to mention two publications. *The History and Antiquities of the County of Dorset*, by John Hutchins, Dorset parson and historian, an eighteenth-century monumental work of scholarship, with Volume III of this four-volumed work covering Gillingham and the surrounding area in minute detail. Hutchins used a variety of primary sources ranging from the local vicar, William Newton, who had been incumbent of the parish from 1696 to his death in 1744, to an extensive documentary use of pipe rolls, now in the PRO. However, *Gylla's Hometown (1983)*, by Charles Howe, might prove a better starting point as it is more accessible.

IWERNE COURTNEY or SHROTON
– North Dorset

South of Shaftesbury. On the A350, Shaftesbury to Blandford section. O.S. Landranger 194.

Dedicated to Saint Mary

'Shroton, Shrewton, Shereveton, alias Ewern Courtney, a large parish, situated in a vale, on the little River Ewern, from which it takes its principle ancient name, and its additional one from the Courtneys, once lords of it.' Thus runs the opening passage for Shroton in John Hutchins' *The History and Antiquities of the County of Dorset*. The name Shroton was thought to be a 'nick-name', but Shroton is a corruption of *Sheriffstun* from it once having belonged to Baldwin the Sheriff, listed in the *Domesday Survey*.

To the compass west of the village and looming over it, is Hambledon Hill, one of the regional west's most massive hill-forts which, during the Iron-Age, formed a major settlement for the Belgic tribe; the Durotriges. It is still spectacularly impressive, with easily discernible huge earthen ramparts, maze-like entrances and multiple ditch systems. As heavily fortified as it was, the fort was completely overrun by the Roman General Vespasian's legion, the second Augusta, in AD43.

In August 1645 Hambledon Hill was overrun again, although in smaller numbers, by Cromwell's Parliamentarian troopers, under Major Desborough who, '… came down like a wolf on the fold,' (to use Lord Byron's line in *The Destruction of Sennacherib*) to execute, round-up and suppress the 'Dorset Clubmen' who had made a stand against Cromwell on the hill's plateaued summit.

The rebellion was brought about because of the turmoil of the English Civil War. The Clubmen were fed-up with having their farms overrun by troops, who also stole their goods and cattle, and generally wrought havoc upon the countryside. The Clubmen appear to have had no fixed allegiance to either Royalist or Parliamentarian causes, although there were some who wished to be shot of the Royalists. Mass meetings were called; one in particular, at Badbury Rings, where four thousand gathered armed with clubs, swords, pitchforks and firearms at which Thomas Young, a lawyer from Manston, announced their proposals. Some of their battle-standards carried the unequivocal message:

If you take our cattle,
We will give you battle.

A similar meeting was called at Sturminster Newton, with petitions for both Royalists and Parliamentarians. Cromwell and Fairfax, the Commander-in-Chief of the Parliamentarian army, were encamped at Sherborne where they planned to attack the castle. When Fairfax moved on Dorchester, a number of the Clubmen's leaders met him, only to be told that by forming an army and acting by force, they were acting illegally; Fairfax warned them of the consequences should they continue. However, continue they did and a number gathered on Shaftesbury Hill. After Cromwell's dragoons were ordered up they seized around fifty of the leaders, including Robert Rocke, Rector of Chettle, described as a 'desperate malignant' – probably meaning a Royalist parson. The Clubmen continued their resistance on the hill in Shaftesbury when Cromwell, it would appear, politely asked them to send their leader to talk to him; their reply was to fire on his soldiers.

On 4 August, two to four thousand Clubmen gathered on Hambledon Hill (secondary accounts, which have probably gained from the telling and re-telling of the saga, all differ relating to the numbers involved). It was this gathering which Major Desborough and his troopers attacked, falling on the rebels from Hanford, having been led to that side by an alleged traitor. The majority of the rebels ran off but around sixty were killed, their bodies later being buried to the south of the west tower in St Mary's churchyard. A further two to three hundred were caught, including four rectors and their curates; all were incarcerated overnight in the church, no doubt fearing the worst come the following morning. Cromwell wrote to Fairfax, 'Many are poor silly creatures, whom if you please to let me send home they promise to be very dutiful for time to come.' They were duly released except Thomas Bravell, rector of Compton Abbas, and a number of other ringleaders. It was the end of the Dorset Clubmen's rebellion.

The uncomplicated, eleven feet square, Perp. period W. tower of the late fourteenth century (with alterations in the seventeenth century) has characteristic short diagonal buttressing, simple trefoil-headed louvred bell-openings and an embattled top stage. The chancel, also of fourteenth-century origin, was remodelled in the seventeenth century; other interior alterations were carried out in 1872. The rest: nave, N. aisle and S. chapel were built in the Gothic style by Sir Thomas Freke in 1610. In 1871 the S. aisle and a solid, handsome S. porch were added, the latter being improved in 1962.

In the tower is a ring of six bells: the tenor, inscribed, *To the glory of God and in memory of Queen Victoria's Jubilee 1887*; number 5, inscribed *Santa Maria*, is probably Pre-Reformation; number 4, *Geve thanks to God IW 1590*; number 3, recast by Mears and Stainbank (now the Whitechapel Bell Foundry); number 2, probably 1613 and the treble bell 1920. The RCHM's 1972 report on Shroton, recording only four bells, followed Hutchins, which was by then out of date.

There is some attractive stained and painted glass in St Mary's all of which, with one exception, is Victorian. The exception is a head *c.*fifteenth/sixteenth centuries, set in a roundel in the upper tracery of a window on the N. side of the chancel. The E. window, dedicated in 1870 to Emily Prother, is a three-light depiction of the life of Christ: on the left is the Birth, in the centre is the Crucifixion and on the right is the Ascension. But the one outstanding work of art and craftsmanship in the chancel is the highly unusual and distinctive altar reredos, presented to St Mary's in 1889. It is moulded from Doulton Ware terracotta which, according to the church notes, was made in a local pottery managed by Lady Baker who designed and modelled a large part of it herself. The head of Christ in the centre panel is a typically Victorian depiction. The Victorian encaustic floor tiles in the chancel and sanctuary are in very fine condition which, according to their design, probably came from the Herbert Minton factory. *(See Upton Noble.)*

As related above, Sir Thomas Freke, then patron of Shroton, rebuilt the nave, N. aisle and S. chapel in 1610. The Freke family, originally small farmers, arrived in Iwerne Courtney during the late fifteenth century. Robert Freke (d.1592) rose to a degree of prominence as auditor and teller of the Exchequer under Henry VIII and Elizabeth I; as a result he was able to considerably expand his estate.

For those interested in the science and art of heraldry, the memorial to Sir Thomas Freke (b.1563), (sometime MP for Dorset) situated at the end of the N. aisle is a brilliant object lesson. It stands, floor (under which is the Freke vault) to roof, sited in what is described by Hutchins as a Memorial Chapel. The memorial, in all its polychromatic glory, is enclosed by beautiful carved parclose screens; the one in the N. aisle is adorned with numerous carved 'bulls heads, chained' (the Freke crest), set within the tracery panelling. The other screen, separating the chapel from the chancel, bears the Taylor arms; Sir Thomas married Elizabeth Taylor. He died in 1633 aged seventy and Lady Elizabeth, in 1641, aged seventy-four. The monument was erected by their surviving sons, Raufe and William, in 1654. The central panel of slate, the lettering now somewhat illegible, carries a lengthy inscription and commences, 'To the happy memory of Sir Thomas Freke Kt eldest son of Robert of Shroton esq. and of Elizabeth, his wife, only child of John Taylor of Burton [Bradstock] esq.[merchant and alderman of London].' Those interested in a complete reading of the text and the full pedigree of the Frekes of Shroton should consult Hutchins.

The official blazon, or description, of the Freke Achievement, taken from the Heralds' Visitation of Dorset in 1623, is as follows:

Arms:

Sable, two bars, and in chief three mullets or.

Crest:

A bull's head couped at the neck sable, horned or.

On both sides of the inscriptive panel on the monument are five shields which display the arms and matches (marriages) of Sir Thomas and Lady Freke's children. The church notes record that the stars and stripes (mullets and bars) of the sons are on the left side of the shields and those of the girls are on the right. The stars and stripes are reputed to have been the inspiration for George Washington, (1732–1799) who incorporated them into the flag of the United States of America when one of the later Freke daughters married into the Washington family.

Another prominent local family, the Bakers are well represented in the church by a number of memorial tablets, most of them situated in the S. aisle and in what now appears to be only a nominal chapel, with a single parclose screen at its W. end. The three Victorian windows in the aisle are also dedicated to members of the family. *(For a full pedigree see Hutchins.)*

One of the tablets recording Sir Randolf Littlehales Baker (1879–1959), the last Baronet of Ranston, is also dedicated to his wife Dame Elsie. (The Littlehales became part of the Baker family and their Arms are also shown in Hutchins, alongside the Bakers.)

There are a number of floor-slabs dedicated to the Ryves, another prominent local family, whose pedigree is, again, listed in Hutchins.

St Mary's, Shroton is an ideal place for visitors who wish to escape, even for a brief period, the perplexing complexity of contemporary life and to pray and contemplate an older, ordered and elegant England, taking comfort from Psalm 62:6 to which attention is drawn on the Freke monument:

He only is my rock and my salvation,
He is my defence; I shall not be moved.

Authorised Version

KILMINGTON
– South-West Wiltshire

Off the B3092, north-west of Mere.
O.S.Landranger 183.

Dedicated to Saint Mary

Whit Sunday morning 1557, here in Kilmington, saw the direct confrontational beginnings of an already well established feud, which led, ultimately, to the terrorisation of a family and a mob-driven murder of two men, William and John Hartgill. Almost a year later some of those involved and found guilty of the repugnant and execrable crime, were executed. Charles, the eighth Lord Stourton was hanged in Salisbury, with one final comfort, a silken rope. Four of his accomplices were hanged in Mere and other places; lacking the nobleman's privileged concession.

The church notes draw attention to the fact that in 1791 St Mary's was described as being, '... very neat ... though in the illustration of that date on the wall near the font it looks rather shabby.'

The first Rector, William de Ludeford, appointed in 1338, performed his ministry in what was the first church here; the only extant remains being the arch near the organ and the tower. In a description of the church in general Revd W Phelps apologetically recorded in 1837, 'The tower is a humble copy of the one at Bruton.' Thirty years on in 1867, a more bullish tone can be detected in the making of a rather blunt pronouncement about their village church, by an unknown connoisseur who put their feelings in writing, '... barn would be too good a word for it.' The then newly appointed Rector, Revd Mark Warburton, clearly incensed by so forthright an agrarian appraisal, set forth to restore the nave, demolish the Hartgill

Chapel, build the N. aisle and enlarge the old porch. A doorway was blocked and a new entrance was made near the tower, a fashionable practice at the time, according to the notes. The Rector, still aflame, saw to it that the church had a new font and a neat tower screen of pitch pine erected. However, he was not completely satisfied until a warming apparatus had been installed. Now just in case anyone, local or otherwise, thought that he may not have done enough for St Mary's the Rector then stumped up £500 out of his own pocket to pay for the alterations; £500 out of a total cost of £1,300.

Along came the Bishop of Oxford in December 1868 to re-open the building, no doubt at the invitation of the, by now £500 worse off Rector who, no doubt, hoped to bask in the warm glow of praise and appreciation which would surely be heaped upon him. The Bishop in his address had decided to deliver an admonishment to the congregation, 'You know how all this which had passed upon this old house of God by degrees infected the temper of the people in it and led to it being a house of strife instead of a house of love.' The Rector may well have been pleased, so far, with the Bishop's remarks. However, the senior cleric then took something of a verbal swipe in the direction of the Rector by declaring, 'You remember those terrible high pews which separated one worshipper from another, pews which, with changing taste, we should probably now admire and which kept out the draughts.' The Rector appears not to have been unduly upset because he remained here until his death in 1910.

The three stage, battlemented and pinnacled W. tower, c.1420, built by Sir Richard Bray, rises to sixty feet. The S. face has two niches with figures, replaced in 1906; one, St Mary the Virgin, the other the Archangel Gabriel. This work was carried out as part of a general restoration of the tower by Charles E Ponting (1850–1932) who was Diocesan Architect of Salisbury. The W. door has an attractive four-light window above. The bell-stage originally had a ring of four bells, but two became damaged and were sold in 1782 as scrap metal. A third was sold in 1967 and the remaining bell, which according to the church notes cannot be rung, is beaten by hand with a clapper. Access to the bell-stage is via the stair turret from inside the church tower.

The chancel originally had no E. window opening, but following a rebuilding in 1863, windows were added. The three light E. window, which now exists, was donated in 1878 by Ann Warburton, wife of the Rector, in memory of her own father. This Late Victorian Period window positively swims with jewelled colour. The two windows on the S. side of the chancel are by Cox & Son of London who specialised in this style of window. They were usually chosen from a pattern book and then personalised by the addition of the name of the person to whom it was dedicated. An inscription marks the grave of the Revd Richard Potter, Rector from 1598–1626. A mathematician and Member of the Royal Society, he is credited with being one of the first to experiment with the principles of blood transfusion. A further memorial in the chancel is the donation of an 'all seasons' altar frontal, by Mrs Marriott, in memory of her husband, an England Team cricketer, who died in 1966. At the Kennington Oval in 1933 he took all West Indian wickets with his leg-spin bowling for 96 runs. A talented gentleman from a now lost golden age.

The very beautifully carved pulpit, with shields and gilded angels, was donated in 1911, by Charles Camborne-Paynter in memory of his wife.

The E. end of the N. aisle, built in 1867, was formerly the site of the Hartgill Chapel. The notes suggest that it is likely that numerous members of the family are buried here including the two who were murdered. The very attractive E. window was erected in 1869 by Henry and William Hartgill as a memorial to their murdered ancestors.

One cannot leave St Mary's, Kilmington without recalling those desperate events which led to dual murder. A long-standing feud existed between Lord Stourton of Stourton House, where Stourhead House now stands, and William Hartgill who lived at Kilmington Manor House, which is on the right as the visitor enters the churchyard.

At the Dissolution of the Monasteries the Stourton family (*see Stourton*) acquired the Manor of Kilmington, which had belonged to the Abbey in Shaftesbury; William Hartgill was the tenant when the Abbey still functioned. William the seventh Lord Stourton, Deputy-General for King Henry VIII at Newhaven, left his wife and children to live at the Manor House in the care of William Hartgill, still managing the estate, while he went off to Newhaven to be with his mistress Agnes Ryce. Later, the two of them left to live in France. On his death in 1548 William, Lord Stourton, left a large portion of his estate to his mistress; the rest to his son Charles, eighth Lord, *but nothing* to his wife who was still living at the Manor House under the care and expense of William Hartgill. Hartgill, already accused of mismanagement of the seventh Lord's affairs, was dismissed by Charles. However, when Hartgill sought a maintenance allowance for the upkeep of the Dowager Lady Stourton in 1557, the whole miserable affair reached a point of crisis.

On Whit Sunday morning 1557 Lord Stourton arrived in Kilmington with a large number of men bearing bows and guns. John Hartgill, William's son, warned of Stourton's approach, drew his sword as he emerged from the church and ran to his father's house. A number of arrows were fired at him but he remained unharmed. William, his wife and some servants ran towards the church having decided to seek refuge in the tower. John Hartgill drove away Stourton and the mob from the house and some from the church. He then went into the house and emerged carrying a longbow and arrows and a woman was pressed into carrying a crossbow and gun for him. However, ten others of the mob remained in the church, one of whom John shot in the shoulder. When they had all fled John asked his father what to do. The old man's advice was that he should ride to the court (possibly Frome) and inform the council of events. Food and drink were hoisted up the tower for those inside and the son rode off. On the Monday evening he related to the council what had transpired and how his father had been dealt with by Stourton. On Wednesday the High Sheriff of Somerset, Sir Thomas Speke, was despatched to rescue the captives and commit Stourton to London's Fleet Prison.

Stourton was ordered to pay damages to the Hartgills and on 11 January 1558, around 10am, he arrived to meet them, unfortunately bringing a mob of sixty men with him. William and John Hartgill, on seeing this mob, became understandably alarmed. They were physically seized and dragged to the church house, (the notes suggest a kind of Parish Hall) west of the church, robbed and taken to the Rectory. The same night the Hartgills were murdered, in the presence of Lord Stourton, in a cellar at Stourton House. Lord Stourton was hanged in Salisbury Market Place on the 6 March 1558. There are at least two divergent accounts of the above narrative the details of which have, in this case, been taken from the current church notes. A slightly different version can be found in the guide book, *Stourhead*, published by the National Trust.

It is very likely that this church will be locked. The key may be obtained from the farm opposite the W. door.

LANGHAM
– North Dorset

*Just off the A3081, immediately west
of Gillingham. O.S.Landranger 183.*

Dedicated to
Saint George

Although St George's is not a parish church, the only exception in this volume, it is one well worth visiting. This church is a memorial to those young men of the community around the hamlet of Langham, who, in the lofty language of the inscription on a bronze wall plaque, 'Left all that was dear to them, endured hardness, faced danger, and finally passed out of the sight of men.' One could not say with certainty that this church is unique, in that there may be others built to express the profound shock at the carnage and death toll of so many young, vibrant lives which Britain experienced during and following World War I.

Alfred Manger retired from banking and entrepreneurial activities in Hong Kong and London in 1890. Following his retirement he lived at Stock Hill House, Langham. It had long been his intention to build a church on his land, for the spiritual benefit of the employees on his estate, and for the hamlet of Langham. As European events developed, it evolved into a memorial to the sacrifices made by so many during the First World War in which he, like millions of other British families, lost close family members; his son, nephew and son-in-law. Manger died in 1917 before his plans could be put into effect but his widow decided that he should be interred at the location where the church was to be erected. His intention to build a church was directly fulfilled by his son, Lt Col Charles Harwood Manger MC. The finished church was dedicated to St George, on Trinity Sunday, 22 May 1921, by the Bishop of Salisbury. Alfred Manger's noble concepts and the church's design are simple; as the great Greek historian Thucydides observed, 'The simple way of looking at things is so often the mark of a noble nature.'

St George's, situated W. of Gillingham, between Wyke and Buckhorn Weston, is indisputably a rural building, bringing to mind an Anglo–Saxon England. It was designed by Charles E Ponting, Diocesan Architect of Salisbury, who received his inspiration from the thatched church at Freshwater Bay, Isle of Wight. (Ponting's best work can be seen in his design for St Mary's, Fordington, Dorchester [1910–12].) St George's is built from warm Ham stone, the only architectural variation being in the broken arched Gothic clear glazed lancet windows. Importantly, it is one of the very few thatched churches in England and, suggest the church notes, possibly the only one built in the twentieth century.

It has an apsidal E. end and a small semi-circular recess, acting as a vestry, in the N. wall. The internal walls are of ashlar blocks of Ham stone, the dressing of which brings out the beauty of the subtle colourings ranging from ochre to gold. The furnishings are appropriately simple; wicker seated chairs, plain wooden altar rails, silver candlesticks and the altar, with its unfussy cross drawing the eye, as always in apsidal-ended churches, into a sharp focus.

The spiritual care of the church has always been the responsibility of the Rectors of Gillingham. It is not in frequent use but well attended services are held at Christmas, Easter and Whitsuntide. St George's is managed by a Charitable Trust, run by a Board of Trustees. A 'Friends of St George's' network also exists for the purpose of broadcasting information and attracting new 'Friends'. An occasional Summer Flower Festival is held to raise funds towards upkeep and maintenance, and to visit on such a day is a delightful experience. Imagine … an intensely bright, very hot English Summer's morning, the air heavy with the droning of bees and the perfume of flowers. Imagine … a Merchant-Ivory film; a period costume drama set, say, in the 1930s, the panama hats and linen jackets, the large-brimmed, chiffon-trimmed straw hats, elegant floral print dresses, light-hearted chatter and quiet laughter of the English on parade, taking their ease against a backdrop of a tiny stone-built church in a small tree-lined and sheltered churchyard …

LONGBRIDGE DEVERILL
– South-West Wiltshire

On the A350 Shaftesbury to Warminster road.
O.S.Landranger 183.

Dedicated to
Saint Peter and
Saint Paul

Undoubtedly the best route to Longbridge Deverill is through the village of Mere. Once through the village the gradient rises sharply and it is a stiff climb to the top, but what a view upon reaching it! Looking down over the Blackmore Vale the vista is truly spectacular. On the way up do try to glimpse, on the right hand side, the lynchets on the chalk face of Mere Down. Lynchets were medieval and later intensive strip farming on hillsides, which attempted to use all available cultivable land.

The road from Mere passes through a succession of Deverill villages: Kingston Deverill has the church of St Mary the Virgin, superbly sited on a right-angled bend; Monkton Deverill with its redundant church of St Alfred the Great; Brixton Deverill, where Alfred the Great reputedly prayed on the eve of battle against the Danish King Guthrum whom he fought at Edington AD878, has St Mary's Church; Hill Deverill, has another redundant building, The Church of the Assumption; and finally into Longbridge Deverill. All these ancient villages either run parallel with or dwell astride the River Wylye (OE – tricky stream). Turn left from the B3095 onto the A350. Climbing modestly towards Warminster, the church of St Peter and St Paul is on the right, at the northern end of the village. Down the very narrow lane on the right is the church car park.

The church has a powerful physical presence. The fourteenth-century W. tower is square and solid and because it lacks ornate architectural refinement, its sharply defined squarely embattled top, with no pinnacles, has a militarily fortified aspect to it. The only extravagance is in the above-tower stair-turret capped with a polygonal spirelet and topped with a golden cockerel wind vane. (The symbol of the cockerel is Vigilance. Vane is a corruption of the original French *fane* from the word *fannion*; a banner.) St Peter and St Paul's defies its surroundings, having been somewhat displaced by progress (the busy and wide A350 passes within fifty feet or so), therefore it has lost its original context and its position of dominance on the eastern facing slope of the hillside. However, its assurance remains. The entire building is unquestionably handsome and sturdy; the very stones of the fabric speak of good health. Looking further around the exterior, the tower has a large Perp. period W. window, but the louvered bell-openings are Dec. period. A departure from what could be seen as conventional, the N. and S. aisles possess their own pitched roofs. The E. window and NW window are Victorian, the rest are straight-headed Perp. period. The oldest portion of the existing building is the Norman N. aisle of the mid-twelfth century. The re-built S. aisle is fourteenth century.

In AD986 Wulfhelm, Saxon Archbishop of Canterbury, granted the Manor of Longbridge Deverill to the Abbot of Glastonbury. King Aethelstan, who ruled from AD924 to his death in AD939, a generous donor to churches both in England and in Europe, certified the grant by charter, and the Abbot of Glastonbury held the manor until the Dissolution in 1539. The church notes, compiled by the Deverill Valley History Group, state that it is likely that a wattle church stood on this same site, before the existing building, its presence attested by the *Domesday Survey* of 1086.

In the interior, the N. arcade has three bays of unmoulded Romanesque arches with square piers built from ashlar blocks. The fourteenth-century S. aisle has a chamfered Gothic arched three-bay arcade. The chancel, with a two-bay arcade into the Bath Chapel, is Victorian, *c*.1860. The high fourteenth-century tower arch accommodates the church organ perfectly and the three-light W. window, above, is of clear glazed white glass. Whilst above them all, in the tower, hangs a ring of eight bells. The oldest, currently in use, of

1614 bears the inscriptive initials *RP* (Purdue). The tenor bell was cast with the inscription, *Peace and Prosperity to this Parish 1739.*

The original Manor House stood on the north side of the church and in 1547 it was the home of Sir John Thynne. Sir John was present at the Battle of Pinkie in the same year, when he was Seneschal (a flexible title, probably Steward) to Edward of Somerset, then Lord Protector of England. It was Sir John Thynne who built Longleat House. Thomas Thynne (1734–96) was created first Marquess of Bath, and held important offices during the reign of King George III.

Longleat House was once within the parish of Longbridge Deverill and the Thynne Family Vault lies beneath the Bath Chapel on the N. side of the church. The chapel was added in 1852 when other restorations were being carried out. The Ludlow altar tomb was placed in this chapel having been brought here from the Church of the Assumption at Hill Deverill when that church was made redundant in 1984. Lieutenant General Edmund Ludlow was one of Cromwell's Parliamentarian officers and a signatory to the Death Warrant of King Charles I. The church notes point out the irony that the Royalist Thynnes and the Parliamentarian Ludlows should be brought together in this fashion, after occupying adjacent territories and viewing each other with veiled hostility during those times. A holy water stoup also stands in the centre of the chapel. A most astonishing furnishing which stands at a height of over eight feet; it makes no concession to modesty. The stoup is made from bronze with an alabaster bowl and access to the holy water is made by lifting one of the four ornate covers in the upper bowl. This unusual furnishing was donated by the family as a memorial to Lord John Thynne who was killed whilst riding in 1882. Originally, on the topmost section, stood a silver figure which has, unfortunately, been missing since 1902 when it was stolen whilst the stoup was being returned from an exhibition in London. The entire work was designed by Sir Alfred Gilbert, (1854–1934) who was responsible for the statue of Eros in Piccadilly Circus. Pevsner declared the stoup to be, ' … one of the few things in England that corresponds to Gaudi's work in Spain.' It certainly reveals traces of Art Nouveau influence, a flamboyant style which was making an impact around that time in Europe including England. Gilbert studied in London, Paris and Italy; more of his work is in St George's Chapel, Windsor. On the W. wall of the chapel are a number of military accoutrements, allegedly, relating to Sir John Thynne including a tilting helm worn by him at the Battle of Pinkie. There is a memorial tablet dedicated to Sir John on the lower portion of the S. wall of the Bath Chapel. The chapel parclose screens are c.early nineteen-twenties, by Frederick Charles Eden (1864–1944) who worked with Ninian Comper *(see Whitam Friary)* when both were employed by Bodley and Garner, Architects. The windows comprised of diamond or lozenge shapes (known as quarries) are of clear and lightly tinted glass.

What a splendid display of stained and painted glass there is in all parts of the church. The modern Glastonbury window in the N. aisle is comprised of eight sections and tells a story, as in medieval glass, of events, in this case, relating to Glastonbury Abbey. The centre light is of Joseph of Arimathea who, according to tradition, brought Christianity to the west of England. One of the great benefactors of St Peter and St Paul's was Canon Brocklebank. It was he who provided a legacy to fund the stained-glass by Kempe. *(See Donhead St Mary.)* All the clerestory windows in which the figures are well defined, sharp and ideal for viewing from a distance, are by Kempe. There is further work by him in the N. aisle, but it is in the glowing E. window that Kempe's work shines forth. It is his detailed style and palette at its most beautiful. The window was installed in 1931 in celebration of the eight-hundredth anniversary of the church, its main subject being *The Adoration of the Child Jesus by His Mother*, accompanied by angels.

The altar stone has five crosses incised into it. According to the church notes, tradition has it that when Thomas Becket, Archbishop of Canterbury (1118–1170), came to consecrate the church, it was he who carved the crosses. Whatever its provenance, it was discovered in 1858 underneath a path in the churchyard, when work was being undertaken on the chancel. Again according to tradition, it had been hidden in 1662 by the vicar, Revd William Parry, to protect it from Parliamentarian soldiers when they were moving on Longbridge

Deverill. The local traditions relating to Becket are possibly strengthened by a song *(see church notes)* referring to him, which was sung by local children until relatively recently. His visit was, possibly, genuinely remembered in the oral folk memory of local inhabitants.

The richly crafted reredos, behind the main altar is a memorial to Captain Morrice killed in WWI. He was the son of a former rector of Longbridge and Monkton Deverills. The centre tableau depicts the crucifixion and on the right, facing the viewer, is Capt Morrice, St Edmund and St Birinus, the Apostle of Wessex. On the left is St Dunstan, once Abbot of Glastonbury, St Thomas Becket and St George.

On the N. wall of the nave, above the arcading, is a war memorial of a most bold, colourful and unconventional design by F C Eden.

MAIDEN BRADLEY
– South-West Wiltshire

On the B3092, north of Mere.
O.S.Landranger 183.

Dedicated to All Saints

In a beautifully tended, tree abundant, churchyard sits the proudly planted, appealing church of All Saints, with its strongly buttressed W. tower. The ancient Greeks named such a sacred area surrounding a temple the *temenos*, the boundary which separates the profane from the sacred. One feels such an ancient ambience here, after passing through the gates. To walk up the path and feel the hot, high-summer sun on one's face is perhaps to experience a profound and simple pleasure; that of being.

According to the church notes compiled by H D Kitching in 1970, the first written reference to a church here occurs in 1102, but most certainly a church was here in 1066, for both Saxon and Norman remains were found during a period of fourteenth-century rebuilding. The three W. arches of the N. arcade of the nave and the foundations date to *c.*1175. Pevsner points out that there are no visible Norman features. A fourteenth-century wall painting was discovered in 1894 when the wall of the N. aisle was demolished, a coloured copy of which was made by the then incumbent's wife. This currently hangs in the aisle, but all traces of colour have fled.

The nave, chancel, S. aisle, porch and tower are fourteenth-century. The low W. tower has no W. door and has a three-light W. window and clock face, but no battlements. Access to the bell-stage is through the attractive outside stair-turret, *c.*1800.

Alterations to the chancel were made, it is believed, between 1580 and 1610. In 1959 a crypt or vault was discovered near the E. wall. It is likely that it relates to the Ludlow family and is possibly the resting place of a Viscountess of Bindon, buried in 1633. Numerous other alterations were made during the nineteenth century. The choir stalls, and the characteristic floor tiles are from that period. The E. window did possess coloured glass until 1890 when it was removed and replaced. *(See the church notes for further references.)* However, as the chancel window has clear glass, the effect on entering the church on a bright day is quite superb, and the natural light flooding the chancel is a visual delight, contrasting sharply with the darker nave and aisles. The chancel is uncluttered by memorials and is, therefore, outstanding in its simplicity and clarity. The effect of the mid-Victorian glass in the W. window is lost due to the installation in 1967 of the organ in the tower by Lady Susan Seymour, in memory of her parents the Duke and Duchess of Somerset. The simple Lady Chapel in the N. aisle was the original site of the previous organ installed in 1907. In the SE corner of the S. aisle are fragments of glass from the fourteenth and fifteenth centuries and the N. aisle has a window by Christopher Whall dedicated in 1928. Christopher Whitworth Whall (1849–1924), the son of a clergyman, became a major influence on stained-glass not only because of the fine work he produced but also through his teaching. Between 1885 and 1892 he lived near Dorking, where he started his own workshop. His first windows were for St Etheldreda's Roman Catholic church, Ely Place, London in 1879. Unfortunately the church was bombed in WWII but three of his panels survived and are now in the William Morris Gallery in London. Amongst other places, he taught at the Royal College of Art from 1898 and was instrumental in setting up the stained-glass department at Dublin School of Art. Whall worked for the company of James Powell from 1887 to 1894. Some of his other work can be seen, in Gloucester Cathedral and Southall Minster, Nottinghamshire.

All Saints is the fortunate possessor of a number of fine and noble monuments and wall-tablets. In the S. aisle, E. wall is the outstanding memorial to Sir Edward Seymour who died in 1708. He was a Member of Parliament in 1661 and Speaker of the House (1672–78) and is buried in the family vault, rediscovered in 1964; E. end S. aisle. The memorial was erected in 1728 or 1730, sculpted by John Michael Rysbrack who was born Antwerp 1694; settled in England 1720, where he died in 1770. The quality of Rysbrack's work is of the highest artistic order. He has sixteen monuments in Westminster Abbey alone. There is also an equestrian statue in Bristol and many parish churches in England are possessors of his beautiful work. Pyramidal compositions are one of the chief characteristics of his style. Pevsner found the semi-reclining figure of Sir Edward, dressed in the clothes of his age, extremely elegant. Could one disagree?

The nave box-pews, which date from around 1640, were beautifully carved and crafted by 'Walter the Joyner' of Maiden Bradley. St Michael the Archangel, Mere, also possesses oaken nave pews made by Walter, in the same style (but without doors) with turned finials on the bench ends and there are two pews by Walter in All Saints, Fonthill Bishop. The oak pulpit, also Jacobean seventeenth-century, possibly relates to the Restoration. The font of Purbeck marble, standing on four simple pillars is *c*.1200.

All Saints is a church for the visitor to linger over and enjoy, for here is local and national history set on the same stage. 'Walter the Joyner' and the Seymour family are here together.

MERE – South-West Wiltshire

On the B3092, south of the A303(T). O.S.Landranger 183.

Dedicated to Saint Michael the Archangel

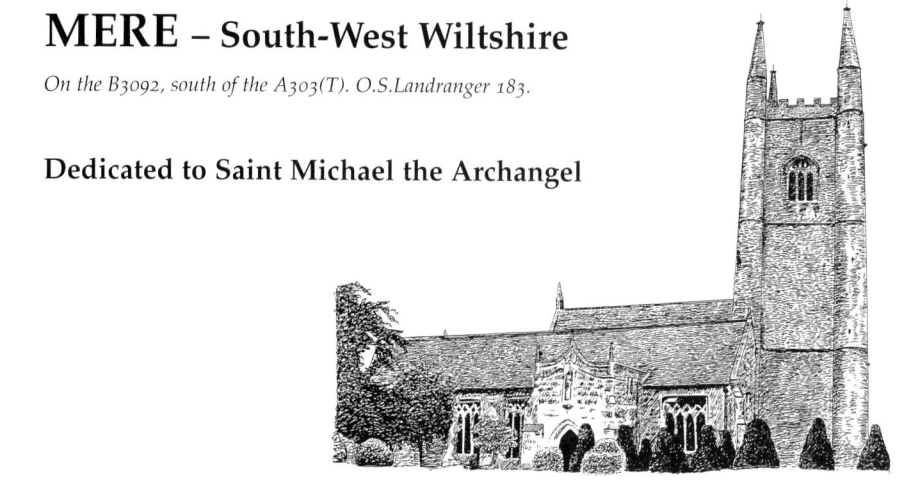

Driving through Mere it would be easy to gain an impression that the village is only a ribbon development. It is not so straightforward. Mere is large and well spread; of great charm and high residential desirability. It was once an important coaching stop, and the hostelries at its centre providing accommodation for travellers are still here and performing their centuries old function. Amongst a number of others is the notable Ship Hotel, Castle Street, (wonderful inn sign!) built as a private house in 1711 and opposite is The George Hotel, built in 1580. Charles II ate here on the 3rd October 1651, after fleeing the field following the Battle of Worcester. The oldest recorded buildings are Woodlands Manor of 1370, Chantry House *c.*1425 and Dewes *c.*1660, all of which are now privately owned. William Barnes, a possessor of many talents but more well known as the dialect poet of this part of the west country, came to Mere in 1823 and set up a school in the Old Market House loft (where the Jubilee Clock now stands). Four years later he married and moved the school to the old Chantry House on the south side of the church. He left here for Dorchester in 1835. *(See Sturminster Newton.)* There is a wealth of other buildings here, and an extended walk around the village will reveal some architectural delights. The best view of the village can be gained from the top of Castle Hill on the north side; look for the flag pole and head for it! As its name suggests there was once a castle on the mound built in 1253 by Richard, Earl of Cornwall. Nothing visible remains but the plateaued top reveals the foundations as a series of bumps under the turf. Celia Fiennes (1662–1741) was an English gentlewoman who travelled all over England at the end of the seventeenth century. She was born in Newton Tony, Wiltshire and was the daughter of a Cromwellian Colonel. During her travels to the West, which She undertook on horseback in 1698, she recorded in her journal that she went from Stonidge *(Stonehenge)* to Evell *(Yeovil)*, ' … thence to Meer a little town; by the town is a vast high hill called the Castle of Meer, its now all grass over and so steepe up that the ascent is by footsteps cut in the side of the hill; I was on the top where some had been digging, and was come to a space that was arched and the walls plaistred and washed white and smooth, it was but a little roome; I tooke a piece of its walls and plaister; that shews there may be cells or vaults in the hill …' The hill is now a WWII Memorial to the 43rd Wessex Division who fell at Hill 112 near Caen, Normandy, in July 1944.

The church of St Michael the Archangel is sited on Church Street, off The Square. Entering the gates the visitor is aware that here is a spacious classic village churchyard landscape. A tree lined path leads to the church and to the right hand side is an avenue of unusual bottle-shaped topiaried trees; the churchyard boundary wall is ringed by picturesque cottages. St Michael's is undoubtedly visually exciting. It is large and noble, particularly the Perp. period tower rising to a height of 124 feet; the very large corner pinnacles each bearing a gilded weather vane, are a spirited flourish. The polygonal buttressing on the north-west and south-west corners suggests architectural class. It is hardly surprising, therefore, that the late, scholarly Sir John Betjeman, a man of style and culture, (sadly missed in a contemporary dumbed-down England) declared St Michael's to be one of the great churches of Wiltshire. Three hurrahs for Sir John!

Even before entering the building there is much to enjoy, as well as the tower. The north porch entrance, of the Dec. period is ornate and superb. In a niche above the door is a statue of St Michael, erected *c.*1160. It is badly eroded, but at least it appears to have remained undamaged by Parliamentarian religious fanatics. The interior of the porch has a fan-vaulted roof.

The nave was rebuilt in the mid-fifteenth century, with the addition of a Perp. style clerestory. The N. side clerestory windows are blank or blind, but the S. side has lights. The roof bosses are nineteenth-century and the fifteenth-century carved angels, which rest on the wall plates, are much restored. The Perp. period nave columns are slender and elegant.

The N. chapel, the church notes inform, is also known as the Still Chapel after a local family, some of whom are buried in the vaults of the church. Nicholas Pevsner states that the chapel was originally a chantry, c.1325; later extended. The N. aisle was widened in the fourteenth century to allow for the chantry chapel alignment, as was the S. aisle for the same reason. The S. chapel, again built originally as a chantry, is known as the Bettesthorne Chapel. Facing the altar, set in a floor of fourteenth-century tiles, is a well preserved brass (unfortunately vandalised) of 1398, dedicated to John Bettesthorne.

Within St Michael's there is a cornucopia of delights – imaginatively artistic and superbly crafted interior furnishings and memorials. For example, the Perp. period rood screen dividing the nave from the chancel is just one such visual gem; it must be one of the finest in the county and perhaps beyond. The Holy Rood section above, is of the late-nineteenth-century. The best of the two chapel screens, or more properly parclose screens, is that of the S. chapel. The choir stalls are comprised of both old and new; the fronts of the stalls have fifteenth-century panels. Do seek out the misericords situated in the rear S. side stalls which are fifteenth-century; compare them with those on the N. side are which are twentieth century. The octagonal Perp.style font is of Purbeck marble. Note the splendid pews of 1640 which were made by Walter the Joyner of Maiden Bradley. All Saints of Maiden Bradley has a similar set of nave pews, but with doors, made by the same talented Walter. (There are also two pews at Fonthill Bishop in Walter's unmistakable style.)

Most of the stained-glass is Victorian and some of it may be from the continent however, the most outstanding window of this period is the N. aisle, W. window of 1865, by one of the finest and most expensive of all Victorian stained-glass artists, Henry George

Alexander Holiday (1839–1927). It is likely that the S. aisle, W. window is also by him. Holiday became a disciple of Burne-Jones and it was during his training at the Royal Academy Schools that he became enamoured of the Pre-Raphaelites. Martin Harrison in his outstanding scholarly work *Victorian Stained Glass*, describes how the company of James Powell and Sons of Whitefriars asked Holiday to become their chief designer to replace Burne-Jones, which he did in 1863, and continued to work for them until 1891 when he founded his own workshop. The window here of *Faith, Hope* and *Charity* (separate lights) is from the days of his early association with James Powell. This window shows Pre-Raphaelite influence, which he eventually left behind when he became inspired by Classical Greek art. Holiday had a long career in stained-glass design which lasted from 1863–1926. The reason he opened his own workshop was that he became increasingly dissatisfied with the quality of Powell's work. He closed his own studio in 1914 and went to another manufacturer. Powell remained in business until 1973. In the S. wall is a modern etched white-glass window by J H Finnie dated 1983. Finnie's speciality is as a designer of etched glass.

There is such a wealth of quality furnishings in St Michael's that it merits either a long, or several short visits but either way, the discerning and aware visitor will find much to treasure. St Michael's is a church not to be missed, it is lovingly and sensitively maintained and cherished. A key to a fuller understanding and appreciation of this wonderful building is to be found in the excellent and well researched guide book by Revd W H V Elliott, revised by Dr D Longbourne, available from the Friends of St Michael book stall in the N. aisle.

MILBORNE PORT
– East Somerset

On the A30 Shaftesbury
to Sherborne road.
O.S.Landranger 183.

Dedicated to Saint
John the Evangelist

Milborne Port has an active village life, as those who live here know. For those who do not, the best publication to consult would be the *Milborne Port Magazine*. If there was a Best Church/Village Magazine Award then this magazine would be high on the list. It is lively, thought provoking, contemplative, informative and humorous. Local businesses support it; local churches of all denominations are kept informed of what each is doing. It even has a regular feature on a subject close to the hearts of the English – the weather! Recipes follow clog dancing and Historical Society meetings; education and informed debate is encouraged through an Adult Education Programme at Wells Cathedral. There are lectures by visiting speakers and there is group exploration of Christianity. As a counterbalance to all the foregoing earnest endeavours there are self-mocking cartoons with a religious flavour and a section which is headlined *Gospel Gaffes*, allegedly taken from school exam papers. A few examples of classic howlers will surely entertain: 'Jesus was born because Mary had an immaculate contraption,' or 'When Mary heard she was the mother of Jesus she sang the Magna Carta,' or 'The epistles were the wives of the apostles,' and finally 'It was a miracle when Jesus rose from the dead and managed to get the tombstone off the entrance,' and so on. Taking all this into account it should hardly come as a surprise to learn that there is a public house named *The Tippling Philosopher*. The village appears to be a miniature Athens of the fifth and fourth centuries BC; the Athens of Socrates, Aristotle and Plato (the thinkers) and Aristophanes (the comic dramatist).

The concept of a Saxon burgh by implication signifies a fortified place of defence but boroughs were also commercial centres. Alfred the Great (AD849–899) established a burghal system as part of an attempt to defend his kingdom and it is likely that Milborne was one such. The suffix, Port, gave it an official status as a trading centre. The church notes by Revd Edmund Digby Buxton, Vicar here from 1954 to 1974, and revised in 1996 by S G McKay, record that coins were minted here, verified by some which exist in national collections, from the reigns of Aethelred II (AD978–1016) and Cnut (AD1016–1035).

There are a number of references to Milborne Port in the *Domesday Survey* of 1086 where it is identified as *Meleburne* and *Mileburne*; a number of mills are recorded. The land was held by King William. A very interesting entry, possibly relating to earlier minting activities, refers to £80 of blanch silver less 9 shillings, 5 pence. The church is shown as being held by Regenbald (possibly the priest), with 1 hide of land and 1 plough. Milborne Port's importance is, therefore, well established.

Arriving at the church along a quiet lane at the west front, the first view of this large, dignified building set in a spacious churchyard, is undoubtedly uplifting. It promises great visual pleasure; upon closer examination it does not disappoint.

St John the Evangelist bears very visible and outstanding evidence of differing architectural periods; Saxon, Early Norman, fifteenth-century Gothic, and Victorian. It is suggested that a visitor, before entering the building itself, makes an examination of the exterior, particularly on the south side, where the nave, outside stair-turret and south transept join; it is a triple architectural delight.

Towards the W. end of the exterior wall of the S. nave is a particularly striking Norman doorway. It was restored and heightened in 1843 and the quality of its carving and lack of weathering should be taken into account when appreciating its craftsmanship. Above the door in the tympanum, or pediment, are two intricately carved ferocious animals, believed to be original. The whole doorway with its Romanesque arch is in an unmistakable Norman style; worth travelling to see. The window to the right of the door is fifteenth-century. Moving east, in the corner angle, is the stair-turret faced with square stone slabs placed in a diamond pattern, along with three string-course layers. Standing next to the tower, the W. wall of the S. transept has a small original Norman window above the string-course, continued along from the stair turret. The S. window is late thirteenth-century with renewed tracery. Around the corner from the S.transept is the S. wall of the chancel, the oldest part of the building. The windows are comprised of one single-light and a lower, double-light of the thirteenth-century; a three-light window is in the Dec. style of the fourteenth-century, as is the small, priest's door.

The chancel interior bears a number of Saxon hallmarks in its construction, particularly the S. wall. There was a window in the N. wall which is only visible from within, revealing that it was once set in an exterior wall. The E. window is also Dec. period and the stained and painted glass of 1908 is by William Bainbridge Reynolds (1855–1935). (There is a fine lectern by the same artist in St Michael's Chapel, Canterbury Cathedral.) On the E. wall, either side the window are niches now installed with two modern figures. In the N. niche is St John the Evangelist and in the S. niche, St Mary and the infant Jesus. The sculptures, from 1972, are by the internationally renowned John Skelton MBE (1923–1996). Skelton was the nephew and pupil of Eric Gill (who executed, for example, the Prospero and Ariel figures on Broadcasting House, London). Skelton trained at Coventry School of Art and some of his works are in Chichester Cathedral and the Bodleian Library, Oxford. The figures have not been sited to their best advantage, as they appear to the onlooker as rather estranged from each other, looking outwards and away from what, surely, should be their focus – the altar and the crucifix. One must ask, therefore, if they are in the wrong niches?

The crucifix and candlesticks, contemporary in style, are by J A Cross of King Arthur's School, Wincanton. Apart from the E. window of the chancel, other refurbishments were carried out in 1908. The roof was added and the very colourful and carved altar frontal (and the pulpit in the nave) redecorated. The altar frontal and pulpit are both in the same style, and have aspects of early Clayton and Bell work. *(See Silton.)*

The nave was almost entirely rebuilt between 1867–9. This included both heightening and lengthening, the latter by twenty-eight feet. The N. transept was rebuilt at the same time and the S. transept refaced.

The tower crossing, a particularly fine feature of St John's, has a combination of Norman Romanesque arching to N. and S. and Gothic arching of the fourteenth century to the E. and W. The original Norman supporting columns still survive and are used for all four sets of arches. Above the arching in the tower crossing is a fifteenth-century coffered ceiling, a feature not often seen in the west of England. Coffered ceilings saw their beginnings in Greek architecture, made from limestone or more elegantly white marble, to reflect light coming up from the floor at, for instance, the entrance to a temple.

The fifteenth-century chancel screen, minus the rood loft but complete with doors, is a surviving feature which we can still appreciate, particularly the delicately carved tracery. The purpose of the screen was to cut off the chancel from the nave. The difficulty for later generations was that they felt excluded from the drama of the celebration of Holy Communion, the celebrant being largely unseen and probably unheard by the communicants. This difficulty has been overcome at St John's by placing an altar and other relevant furnishings forward of the E. arch and into the tower crossing; simple, effective and inclusive. This arrangement also gives the church three areas of worship; the nave, chancel and N. chapel.

The N. chapel is accessible from the chancel through the two-bay arcading. Beneath the floor of the chapel is the burial vault of the Medlycott family, who were great benefactors of the church. The number of bells increased in 1846 from six to eight through the generosity of Sir William Medlycott. In 1908 they were rehung and a new bell-frame installed. One of the bells is inscribed, *Thomas Bilbie made all we*, and on another, *Come here! Friend Knight and Cockey too, such work as this you cannot do.* In 1854 this same William Medlycott also donated land to the church, enabling the churchyard to be extended. Part of this land was never consecrated, due to buildings then standing on it but since demolished. This area is now known as Church Lawn upon which the fine War Memorial was erected in 1921.

The churchyard, like many others, is worthy of exploration particularly with the help of the church guide book.

The interior of the S. transept has a wagon roof whilst underneath its S. window is a very eroded effigy of a Lady, *c*.early-fourteenth-century. The small Norman window in the W. wall *(see the exterior description above)* is worthy of note; its stained-glass lambent with colour.

Of the fine quality stained and painted glass in St John's, some of it is from the eminent studios of Clayton and Bell, in one of their distinctive styles; bold outlines and use of sparkling colour.

The church reflects the importance of Milborne Port past and present. It is a complicated building architecturally and because of that it requires a long visit to be able to appreciate the changes which have taken place over the centuries.

Now, about the two figures in the niches of the chancel …?

PEN SELWOOD – East Somerset

North of the A303 (T), east of Wincanton,
north of Bourton. O.S.Landranger 183.

Dedicated to
Saint Michael
and All Angels

The handsome village of Pen Selwood sits quietly amongst densely wooded country, as it has for centuries. But in the year AD658, the 'Peterborough Manuscript', one of the *Anglo-Saxon Chronicles* documents records that, Cenwalh (643–672), King of Wessex fought against the Welsh near Peonnum. Peonnum has long been recognised as Pen Selwood and the skirmish drove the Welsh westwards as far as the River Parret *(Pedridan)* which was established as the Saxon border. There is evidence of an Iron Age camp in Castle Wood, close to the village, which possibly relates to Cenwalh. (The earthwork is referred to as Keniwilkins castle in the *Anglo-Saxon Chronicles* editor's notes.) In 1016, the very able Danish King Cnut or Canute, obviously having heard by that time that Pen Selwood was a rather quiet place, decided to leave London and venture westwards to engage in battle King Edmund II (Ironside) of Wessex (reigned AD993–1016); a set-to which appears to have been somewhat indecisive. The 'Worcester Manuscript' of the *Anglo-Saxon Chronicles* records, 'King Edmund … rode into Wessex, and all the people submitted to him; and quickly after that he fought against the raiding army at Pen Selwood near Gillingham.' In the first half of the twelfth century other writers were using more developed versions of the *Anglo-Saxon Chronicles*. Some of them are of uncertain authorship – Florence of Worcester, a monk, compiled the *Chronicon ex Chronicis*, an interesting document which reveals a more literary style. In his version of the above event he has Cnut, ' … hastening to Wessex, and gave no time for King Edmund Iron Side *[regi Eadmundo Ferreo Lateri]* to raise his army; however, he met them bravely in Dorset *[Dorsetania]* with the army which he had been able to collect in so short a time, supported by God's help, and engaging them at a place called Pen Selwood *[Peonnum]* close by Gillingham *[Gillingaham]* he conquered, making them to run away.' Ultimately there was an agreed division of the kingdom, leaving Edmund with Wessex and the rest of England to Cnut. King Edmund died the same year and was buried at Glastonbury. Cnut then became King of all England. He died in Shaftesbury on 12 November 1035.

A delightful setting for this attractive, or to quote the church notes, '… comely little church … sits high on a spur of the upper greensand, looking across the Blackmore Vale to the south and to the hills of Camelot and to Glastonbury to the west.' The narrow churchyard path leads down to a small W. door heavily buttressed on either side, with a three-light window above. The low, battlemented W. tower, with gargoyles has an outside stair-turret, accessible from within, leading to the bell-stage, which in turn has simple louvered light openings. The tower has a ring of four bells: number 1, the treble, *In Nomine Domine. Amen*, is pre-reformation; number 2, *Jubilee 1887*, is by Llewellins and James; number 3 (1905) is also by Llewellins and James; number 4, the tenor, *Anno Domine M 1584*, is by George Purdue of Somerset.

The S. porch entrance is composed of a simple archway with a now worn but interesting sculpture *c.*1400 in a niche above which, according to the notes, was brought back from Italy by the incumbent in office between 1841 and 1852. It depicts the Virgin and two kneeling figures. The S. door surround carries characteristic Norman zig-zag carving and the lintel itself shows a lamb within a circle, well guarded by a lion and lioness. The corners carry the carved heads of two kings.

Internally there is an aisle on the N. side, the E. wall of which prominently displays the decalogue, creed and paternoster *c.*1820. St Michael's underwent extensive rebuilding in the nineteenth century. The nave walls were rebuilt and heightened in 1805 and the N. aisle and vestry added in 1848.

One of the artistic glories of this lovely church has to be the pew ends, all of which carry a theme showing medieval figures in the setting of their daily agricultural tasks. They were carved by Clemency Angell in 1927, her 'signature' being the inclusion of a honey bee in some of the scenes. The pews of local wood were made by John Butt of Pen Selwood.

The small and intimate chancel has interesting, deeply recessed, stained and painted glass windows, in the style of Charles Eamer Kempe. The church notes sadly regret that much medieval glass was destroyed in the nineteenth-century renovations. What little there is can be seen in the S. wall.

The simple fine square bowl font is Norman with a modern cover, at the side of which is the finely carved limewood figure of St Michael by Major R K Archer of the parish; its date unknown.

SEMLEY – South-West Wiltshire

South of East Knoyle, south-west of Tisbury. O.S.Landranger 184.

Dedicated to Saint Leonard

The church of St Leonard is situated on the edge of a large open area of common land and if one arrives in Semley from the northern side, especially in high summer when the grass is at its best, the church sits rather like a stately ship becalmed on a sea of green.

In 1866, the date of the rebuilding of St Leonard's, this building along with other even larger establishment churches, particularly those in towns and cities built during the Victorian period, was required to make an impressive architectural statement regarding the status of the Anglican church, to counter the rivalry of growth by non-conformist chapels of many differing shades of sectarian persuasion. This decade and the next two were the apogee of Victorian confidence, 'Whether or not,' observed Owen Chadwick, *The Victorian Church*, 'the citizens attended those churches or chapels, the Victorians preserved a country which was powerfully influenced by Christian ideas and continued to accept the Christian ethic as the highest known to man.' Nevertheless, Victorian society, particularly the churchgoing of whatever persuasion, had been shaken and 'hell's foundations' seemed to 'quiver' somewhat less after Charles Darwin had published his *On the Origin of Species* six years earlier. A N Wilson in *The Victorians* points out, 'Yet if, from the beginning, the Theory of Natural Selection was seen as incompatible with religious belief, much of the blame for this must rest with the churchmen who were too timorous to study the scientific, too lazy to work out the theological implications in sufficient depth. No wonder the perception took root that a choice must be made, aut Darwin, aut Christus, Darwin or Christ.'

If one considers that A N Wilson scores a point against the laziness of Victorian theologians then one should also consider that it may not have been laziness but rather scepticism regarding what science could achieve at that time.

St Leonard's was designed by Thomas Henry Wyatt *(see Fonthill Gifford)* for the Marchioness of Westminster, who lived at nearby Fonthill, and Henry Hall was Rector at Semley (1856–78) when it was still a good time to be an Anglican country parson provided one had a good living with glebe enough. It *is* a large church. The tower, in the Perp. style, is very handsome with a fine well ornamented battlemented top-stage with gargoyles and an unusually high stair-turret capped with a conical spirelet; the bell-stage openings are louvered and ornate. Below them is a four-light W. window.

In the churchyard is an outstanding work of sculpture, a bronze equestrian statue standing about four feet high dedicated to the memory of Lieutenant George Dewrance Irving Armstrong killed in 1915 whilst serving with the Sherwood Foresters Regiment. This miniature bronze of man and horse is superbly detailed. The combination is a timeless and noble concept; both are alert and watchful. This work of 1916 is by Henry Alfred Pegram RA (1862–1937). Pegram was born in London and studied at the West London School of Art and at the Royal Academy Schools from 1881. His work was highly valued; in 1891–2 he designed the relief at the entrance to the Imperial Institute, South Kensington, London and in 1898 a bronze candelabrum for St Paul's Cathedral, London.

Given the attractive exterior there is unfortunately very little in Wyatt's interior on which to wax lyrical. The only monument from the original building is a large thirteenth-century effigy of a priest, under a canopy supported on shafts.

The altar frontal in the S. aisle Lady Chapel is by the North Dorset based artist Joan Salmon ARCA, who trained at Bromley College of Art and the Royal College of Art. It is a beautiful and sensitive work of 1996 depicting the liturgical four seasons. Some of her other work can be seen in Gillingham museum, Dorset where there are a number of display panels including a pictorial reconstruction of King's Court Palace as it may have looked in 1272. *(See Gillingham.)*

There are some fine stained and painted glass windows which make St Leonard's well worthy of a visit. The window in the N. aisle, by F C Eden, is outstanding. Frederick Charles Eden (1864–1944) was born in London, the son of an architect. He trained, along with Ninian Comper *(see Whitam Friary and Longbridge Deverill)*, at Bodley and Garner, a London-based company of architects. In 1910 he started his own studio moving in 1928 to 6, Grays Inn Square, London. The window was made for Eden by Joseph Fisher, whose business address was 50, Rosaline Road, Fulham, London. Eden designed the window in 1897 and it was installed here the following year. The two main figures are Joseph of Arimathea and St Elizabeth of Hungary. The window is in memory of Joseph and Elizabeth Miles to commemorate their marriage at St Leonard's fifty years earlier, in 1848. The couple are represented by miniature figures at the foot of their respective windows. Some of Eden's other work can be found in Chester Cathedral and Wellingborough, Northants. In the S. aisle there is a splendid Victorian, double military window of 1882. One of the panels is dedicated to two brothers, Robert and Guy Glover of the 43rd Monmouthshire Light Infantry, killed in action in New Zealand in 1864; the other panel is to George McDonald, Princess of Wales's Own Regiment, who died in 1881. The windows were designed by William George Taylor (b.1822). Taylor went into partnership in 1873 with William Henry O'Connor, the grandson of the founder of the company Michael O'Connor (1801–1867). Taylor joined them at 4, Berners Street, London, the company address shown on the window. He took over the running of the company in 1877.

However, probably the major reason travellers from far and wide visit Semley, is for the purpose of remembering WPC Yvonne Fletcher (1958–84) of the Metropolitan Police Force, who was mortally wounded by a shot from a window of the Libyan Embassy, whilst on duty in St James's Square, London, during a public demonstration held on 17 April 1984 against the President of Libya, Colonel Qaddafi. In the S. aisle Lady Chapel is a memorial window in her honour. It was designed and made by Henry Haig ARCA (b.1930) of Fifehead Magdalen near Gillingham, Dorset. Haig studied at Wimbledon School of Art and the Royal College of Art where he specialised in stained glass. Some of his other work can be found in Donhead St Mary, Clifton Cathedral, Bristol and Wimborne Minster. The general notes on the church contain an explanation of the window by Henry Haig:

The function of Christian stained glass is unique: to express in visual terms eternal truths through the medium of organised transmitted changing light. Light itself being a constant reminder of the power of God, the light of the universe. By this means it makes a vital contribution to the necessary atmosphere of reflection and prayer within the house of God.

In relation to the theme of the window he writes:

The basic visual form in this instance is direct and simple, gradually revealing through its layers a message of comfort and hope suggesting creation, resurrection and reconciliation expressed in clean freshness to reflect the confidence of youth.

The beginning text for the theme is taken from Psalm 121:1 & 2: 'I will lift up mine eyes unto the hills from whence cometh my help …' A horizon 'hill line' is established across the three main lights to form the suspension point for the central image. This image is generally circular in form expressed as an open flower. This full flower surrounds protectively a young bloom just out of bud, a sign for fresh life developing – a reflection of caring creation….

Within the landscape there are spring flowers to reflect Yvonne's love of the countryside. They are moschatel, primrose, violet, bluebell, wood anemone, celandine, pussy willow and snowdrop. It is intended that the overall 'feel' of the landscape should reflect the character of a mediaeval tapestry.

At the base of the centre light is shown the badge of the Metropolitan Police of which service Yvonne Fletcher was such a proud and valued member. This surmounts her name within the inscription along the base of the three main lights.

This beautifully conceived window by Henry Haig is a delicate tribute to a woman in the flower of her youth; WPC Yvonne Fletcher is rightly honoured and proudly remembered in the memory of the British public not only at the spot in St James's Square where she was killed, but particularly in Semley, where she was born and flourished.

SHAFTESBURY
– North Dorset

At the junction of the A350 & A30.
O.S.Landranger 183.

Dedicated to Saint James

Around AD1300 Shaftesbury had twelve churches and one of the largest and wealthiest Benedictine nunneries in England, with very extensive land holdings and around one hundred and twenty nuns. The town must have been a power-house of tangible spirituality, probably the closest a town in England has come to being a Theocracy; literally, 'The rule of God' – God's will exercised by a priestly order or religious body. In the then prevalent atmosphere of the town, perched as it is on a hill there must have been very little opportunity for the laity to 'err and stray like lost sheep'. Thomas Hardy's comment that, 'Shaftesbury was a place where beer was more plentiful than water, and where there were more wanton women than honest wives and maids,' may have been nothing more than mere levity but may also have contained a fragment of truth; the behaviour a result of the imbalance of centuries before.

Nothing new can be written about the topography of Shaftesbury. The town has been looked up at by many from the foot of the world famous cobbled Gold Hill (named Long Hill on a map of 1615). Whilst the same many have looked down on Gold Hill and the vista beyond, from behind the nineteenth-century town hall and the medieval church of St Peter. Television directors have eulogized and quivered ecstatically over the evocative scene in prospect, one of the most famous 'picturesque' views in England, pondering upon how many loaves of Hovis brown bread this photogenic idyll would sell for their sponsors through a television advertising campaign in 1973. Gold Hill was also used during the filming of Hardy's novel, *Far from the Madding Crowd*. The majestic view has been the subject of many thousands of photographs of 'Ye Olde England', to show the people back home in Alice Springs, Samarkand or Grimsby. Shaftesbury also looks particularly splendid from the air. Aerial photographs show its strong natural position on top of a large four to seven hundred feet, west to east, above sea-level, greensand stone hill overlooking – well, just about everywhere in this part of North Dorset.

Given the prominence and past importance of Shaftesbury it is hardly surprising that a plethora of volumes and published academic papers exist relating to the town, the most recent being John Chandler's, *A Higher Reality*; an excellent overview but more specifically a history of Shaftesbury's Royal Nunnery, written on behalf of the Friends of Shaftesbury Abbey.

Shaftesbury, Thomas Hardy's *Shaston* (not a Hardian invention but the use of an older name) has undergone numerous name changes. The Welsh *Caer Palladur* means the shaft of a spear or pillar whilst *Sceapt* in Saxon means something like the point or end of a hill – a promontory. *Seaftonia, Sceasfstesbyrig, Shafton, Caer Septon* or *Scepton* etc. – the list in Fägersten's, *The Place Names of Dorset* runs to around twenty-six variations of the name.

Whatever the solid facts of occupation, Hutchins declares that, 'Fabulous history attributes a very high antiquity to this town. Some will have Rhudubrasius, or Cicuber, King of the Britons who flourished 940 years before Christ, to have built Palladur or Caer Septon … Holinshed says, it was built by King Lud … Brompton says it was built by Cassibelan, a British King … ' Such is the cloak of high romance which has been draped around Shaftesbury over the centuries.

Although the town occupies a magnificent commanding natural position, no archaeological evidence has yet been discovered to reveal ancient occupation of any significance, apart from debris deposits of flint and pottery in the north-east of the town. It is difficult to conceive, nevertheless, that it was not a fortified settlement considering its position when taken alongside a number of other well-attested local hill-fort settlements; Hod Hill or Hambledon Hill, for example. *(See Iwerne Courtney.)* Occupation most likely began during the Saxon period. In fact the Shaftesbury signs on the approach roads into the centre proudly declare it to be a Saxon Hilltop town.

Shaftesbury's history commences with King Alfred. William Camden, (1551–1623) the English antiquary and pioneer of historical method, thought the town to be undoubtedly built by Alfred. It was part of Alfred's strategic plan, following his victory over the Danish King Guthrum in AD878 at Edington in Wiltshire, to establish a system of burghs – fortified towns – which could be defensive and offensive, in order to protect his kingdom of Wessex.

In very broad terms the Saxon *burgh* occupied the western end of the hill, beginning about half-way along the street named Bimport and moving westwards to where St John's Hill curves left and then plunges steeply. The medieval town lay at the opposite, east end, roughly from where High Street stands, down to Salisbury Street and onwards towards Cann.

William of Malmesbury *(see Bruton)* recorded in his 1125 account of Shaftesbury that an inscription in stone was to be seen, during his lifetime, in the chapter house of the nuns; the stone having been removed from an old wall. Moving forward in time to 1902 a fragment of a stone inscription was found on the site of the abbey church which unfortunately has since been lost. However, very fortunately, a paper-rubbing of the stone fragment was taken around 1904 which is now in the town museum. The fragment of paper shows the remains of the lettering on the stone:

- - - I T •
- - N I C
- A T I O

The RCHM's report on Shaftesbury (1972) states that, based on the conformation of the lettering, the fragment can be dated from *c*.979 to *c*.1050. Allowing for William of Malmesbury's somewhat inexact account, the full inscription, based on the above fragment can be restored as:

AELFRED • REX • HA
NC • URBEM • FECIT •
ANNO • DOMINIC
AE • INCARNATIO

NIS • DCCCLXXX•
REGNI • SUI • VIII
(King Alfred built this town in the eighth year of his reign [AD] 880)

Asser (d.*c*.AD909), a Welsh monk who became Bishop of Sherborne was the enthusiastic biographer of Alfred the Great. He recorded that Alfred built two new religious foundations; one for monks at Athelney in Somerset and one for nuns at the east gate of Shaftesbury. Unfortunately Asser omitted the date when the foundations were established but, following medieval tradition, the year AD888 is the most generally accepted date.

Alfred's abbey of St Mary's was built within a large precinct between the two extremities of east and west. Looking down Gold Hill, the massive buttressed wall on the right – known as Park Wall – is a small remaining section of a wall which originally extended southwards curving all the way to the road called St James at the foot of the hill. The wall continued to curve back up the hill to Bimport. As the name Park Wall suggests its function was to encompass a park which surrounded the abbey, which was possibly used as a deer park and for recreation by the nuns. The western end of the precinct extended to Magdalen (Maudlin) Lane where there were a number of service buildings including a brew-house (near the corner with Bimport) and laundry room. Bordering on Bimport, further buildings included the treasury, other business offices, stables and the main-gate entrance where Abbey Walk now runs. The eastern end of the precinct was on the line of Lyons Walk.

Within the walls of the abbey precinct lay a further sacred building – Holy Trinity Church. The current church of Holy Trinity stands on the same site. This church, which is now redundant, was built in 1841, designed by Sir George Gilbert Scott. *(See Swallowcliffe.)* John Chandler suggests that the original building was probably used by abbey servants as well as the townspeople. The abbey church, including its cloisters built around a central cloister garth, lay to the south of Holy Trinity Church. Of the Saxon abbey there is little or no trace and all that remains of the Norman period edifice, built in the eleventh and twelfth centuries are the impressive foundations, of which there are more further to the west but not exposed. These, together with the well-organised and attractive museum are a must for the visitor. A popular amble in Shaftesbury can be undertaken on Park Walk, given to the town in 1816 by Robert Dyneley, which runs south of the abbey site. On the Walk is the entrance to the abbey site and a weather shelter where one can sit and look south over the broad panorama of the Blackmore Vale. Around the base of the shelter, recorded on glazed tile, is the following text:

> *In the year of the Lord's incarnation 880 King Alfred made this town in the eighth year of his reign. (Inscription recorded by William of Malmesbury circa C12th.) The abbey welcomed pilgrims as this shelter welcomes you. King Alfred ordered the monastery to be built near the east gate of Shaftesbury as a residence suitable for nuns. He appointed as its abbess his own daughter Aethelgifu, a virgin consecrated to God, and many other noble nuns to live with her in the same monastery, serving God in the monastic life …*
> *(Assers' Life of King Alfred AD893.)*

All we can reasonably know about Aethelgifu was that she was the third child of Alfred and, according to John Chandler, was probably little more than in her teenage years when the abbey was founded. It is extremely unlikely that she had no previous experience of monastic life before becoming abbess as she was almost certainly brought up and educated in a religious environment elsewhere in the county of Dorset.

Edward, King and Martyr (*c.*AD963–978), the Peterborough Manuscript of the *Anglo-Saxon Chronicles* tells us, 'was killed in the evening time on 18th March at Corfe "passage" and they buried him at Wareham without any royal honours.' The same manuscript states that two years later, in AD980, 'Here in this year Ealdorman Aelfhere fetched the holy king's body from Wareham and carried it with great honour to Shaftesbury.' There are further versions relating to the events surrounding the regicide of Edward.

John Hutchins, the Dorset parson and historian tells, in the Shaftesbury entry in his *History of Dorset* that, 'This abbey was first dedicated to the Blessed Virgin Mary, but it lost that name, at least for several ages, upon the translation hither of the body of St Edward the Martyr ... on this account the abbey and the church received their names from him; the abbess was styled abbess of St Edward, and the very town almost lost its old name, and was called for sometime *Burgus Sancti Edwardi*, and Edwardstowe. This unfortunate king being esteemed a martyr and canonised a saint, his shrine much resorted to by superstitious pilgrims, and persons of all ranks and qualities, and even by some of our kings particularly by Canute, who died here.' Cnut or Canute died here in 1035 but is buried in Winchester Cathedral.

According to William of Malmesbury portions of Edward's relics were removed to Leominster and Abingdon. Such was the veneration of the Edward cult in the medieval period, more relics of the martyr were despatched to the monasteries of Exeter, York and a number of others. However, in 1931 a startling discovery was made. John Wilson Claridge, son of the new owner of the abbey site, discovered, during a clearing operation in the north transept area, a lead casket under a large stone. In it were human remains, around half a skeleton in all. Claridge believed them to be the remains of St Edward, possibly placed here by the nuns at the time of the abbey's Dissolution. The supposed relics of St Edward remained here until 1951 when the site was sold again. (Anyone interested in developments since the 1950's should read *A Higher Reality*.)

The last abbess of Shaftesbury was Elizabeth Souch, or more likely Zouch, elected to office in 1529. The number of nuns at the Dissolution totalled fifty-six, all of whom received pensions. The end of England's last and largest nunnery came on 23 March 1539 when Elizabeth Zouch signed the document for the surrender of her abbey to John Tregonwell, one of the King's Commissioners.

The shock-waves of disbelief following the Dissolution reverberated through not only the town but also the wider area and may appear to have been devastating. However there are indications that the nunnery was already in serious decline, particularly in relation to the number of nuns which had fallen dramatically. As far as the long-term effects are concerned there have been those who considered that Shaftesbury never fully recovered from Henry's sacrilegious act and all that it involved spiritually and economically. The event was perhaps not quite so devastating as it may appear. Thomas Gerard – a Dorset historian – writing in the 1620s, around eighty years after the Dissolution noted, '… and when that fatall thunder clappe overthrewe the goodlie monasterie and church, it soe shaked the other churches, that onlie foure of them are standing at this daye. Neverthlesse the towne which still remains is a faire thorough faire, much frequented by travellers to and from London; governed by a maior well inhabited and accommodated with a plentifull markett on Saturdayes.' Shaftesbury continued to exist, and not simply to exist but to expand in new directions becoming a major stop for stage-coaches and all that would involve (hotels, horses etc) between London and Exeter in the mid-seventeenth century.

Of the twelve churches in medieval Shaftesbury, only St Peter's, on the High Street, remains. It is a well-attended church much loved by its parishioners and by many visitors to the town. The lane dividing the church from the Town Hall (built 1826) leads down to Gold Hill.

The church of St James is situated in the suburb known as Alcester, a name which may sound familiar as a town in Warwickshire. A William le Boteler of Wemm (now Wem) Salop, gave to Alcester priory an annuity of one hundred shillings which came from the lands and burgages, or rents, in Shaftesbury for the purposes of, 'saying divine service, alms, and other pious works, for the health of his soul and that of the King Henry IV [1366–1413]'. St James' then was in what was known as the Liberty of Alcester. Alcester Abbey was founded in 1140 by Ralph Botiler (sic) of Oversley in Warwickshire, but its interests eventually passed by circuitous legal route to Evesham Abbey. In the reign of Henry VII, St Mary's Abbey paid two shillings a year as ground rent to the abbey of Alcester for use of the land upon which St James' stood.

'The parish of St James stands in a vale south of the town at the foot of Park Hill and St John's, whence issue many little springs that afford plenty of water to this part of the town'; so begins Hutchins' entry for this church.

Thomas Henry Wyatt, in a period of great national church building and rebuilding, was much in demand in the Diocese of Salisbury. Wyatt has received much criticism for his churches and some, but not all, of that criticism has come down from the 1960s when things Victorian became decidedly passé. It is ironic to find that having rid the nation of much fine Victorian work, from the late 1950s and 60s, we have been treated to monumental, mind-numbing, brutalistic architecture in our public and domestic buildings. It is time to look at Wyatt again. There is nothing repetitive or stereotypical in his church designs. All the Wyatt churches are distinctly different from each other; St James' stands in contrast to St Leonard's, Semley, and Holy Trinity, Fonthill Gifford is totally different again.

St James', surrounded by an enclosing wall dating from around 1724, is quite large; it is in the Dec. period style, built between between 1866–7 at a cost of around three and a half thousand pounds and consecrated in August 1867. The building may appear visually heavy, but that is due to the nature of the native Shaftesbury greensand stone from which it is built. The handsome church rises above but does not threaten the close domestic environment. The W. tower, with battlemented top, corner-gargoyles and slender, high, corner-pinnacles replete with sharply carved crockets, (Wyatt loved to add crockets whenever possible) is noble and strikingly elegant. St James' is a splendid example of a suburban, Victorian church. Shaftesbury is clearly a rural town, yet this church has the 'feel' and appearance of Victorian churches to be found in large city suburbs.

Entrance is through the N. porch but before entering, do note one of the few remaining elements from the former medieval building, a fifteenth-century stone parapet which Wyatt positioned above the N. aisle. It has an embattled top, an attractive feature to help break-up and add interest to long straight lines, and immediately below it, carved quatrefoiling. There is a similar parapet above the S. aisle but without an embattled top. It is in the interior where one can still detect the somewhat gloomy and heavy ambience of the building which is how the Victorians liked their churches to look and feel and were fundamental requirements for an environment of spiritual reverence and mystical presence. It is to be hoped that the authentic character is never destroyed. The heavy pews also add their own considerable weight to the pervading atmosphere. It is the perfect church for The Book of Common Prayer and anglo-catholic ritual.

The E. window of 1884 carries no stained-glass artist's mark, its five lights are divided into ten panels, each depicting an episode in the life of Jesus. At the head of the window a roundel shows Jesus triumphant – Christ in Majesty. The carved and painted altar frontal consists of five panels each bearing an image of an angel playing a musical instrument; all are executed in a medieval Italianate style and colouring, providing a fine-art focus for the liturgical ritual. The chancel floor is laid with high-quality, multi-coloured Minton tiles; some of the most well-preserved examples from that maker's factory in the area encompassed by this book.

In the nave are four arcades to N. and S. aisles, the capitals of the columns being generously carved with abundant and luxuriant foliage, all good examples of the standard which Wyatt expected from his masons. The high nave has particularly unusual clerestory windows, each drawn together into a quatrefoil pattern. Around the walls of S. and N. aisles are panels of glazed tiles showing the Stations of the Cross which were made specifically for St James'. The panels are not only unusual but possibly quite rare, executed in the somewhat refined styles of, but not by, Ninian Comper (see Whitham Friary) or F C Eden (see Longbridge Deverill). Little is known of their provenance other than that they were made in London in the 1920s/30s, except Station number XIV. The London company went out of business before completing the set but a Bournemouth company was discovered which completed panel XIV. Hutchins notes that the chancel windows of the medieval church were rebuilt as windows to the aisles and the E. window of the S. aisle, above the chapel altar, was resited here from the same E. position in the chancel. Its stained glass depicts St Peter, St James the Great and St John the Evangelist.

There is a ring of six bells in the tower. The 2nd, by John Wallis, inscribed, *IW 1597 Praise God*; the 3rd inscribed, *'Sancte Jacobe Ora Pro Nobis'*, in Lombardic style lettering of the fourteenth century which, according to church legend, was cast in Shaftesbury; the 4th, by John Danton, inscribed, *'NC, EC, ID, O give thanks unto God 1629'*. The others are from 1875–6. All the bells were re-hung in 1936–7.

Neither Hutchins, Pevsner or the RCHM report of 1972, record the font, sited near the N. door at the W. end of the church, bearing a simple inscription around the bowl, 'John Monde – churchwarden 1664'. It is not original to this church but came here from St Rumbold's, Salisbury Street, when that church was made redundant. It is understood that the Victorian font in St James was disposed of by being broken up and the pieces buried under the church.

To walk down Gold Hill and turn right to St James' would take only a short time and the visitors' efforts would be rewarded by a charming, period church in an attractive setting; built at a time when Queen Victoria, then in deep mourning for her beloved Albert who had died in 1861, had a further thirty-five years in which to wield her influence around the world; when Britain was confident of her premier status in international affairs and confident of God's guiding hand in all things, visible and invisible.

SILTON – North Dorset

*South of the A303(T) and
north-west of Gillingham.
O.S.Landranger 183.*

Dedicated to
Saint Nicholas

'William of Falaise holds Silton *(Seltone)* from the King and Wulfweard held it before 1066.' The Silton mentioned in the *Domesday Survey* (1086), when there were eight villagers, ten smallholders and six slaves, lay in an area near to the present church, on a low ridge between the Stour and a small tributary on the south-west. The present day Silton, divided by the River Stour, is situated on the extreme northern border of Dorset, and St Nicholas' church, built of local limestone and part greensand, lies near the centre of the village. Entering through the handsome new lychgate, erected in 2002, visitors will find themselves in a very spacious and well tended churchyard which, because of its size, has no press of other buildings to disturb or mar its privacy and peace. The nearest other building, by the lychgate, complements the church standing in its own confident and assured space. Passing down the path the broad based fifteenth/sixteenth-century W. tower reveals to the visitor a delightful prospect of an idyllic rural English village church.

The tower is in three stages, with an embattled parapet, small pinnacles, possibly seventeenth-century, and corner gargoyles. Our word, gargoyle, derives from Latin, *gurgulia*, a throat; to gargle. There is no W. door but a simple three-light window punctures the W. wall. The N. side has a small square-headed window. On each face are two trefoil-headed bell-openings of simple design closed by perforated stone slabs. The SE corner carries the stair-turret which leads to the ringing chamber above which is a ring of five bells, the oldest of which, number 3, is probably early-fifteenth-century. Number 2 bell was donated by Judge Hugh Wyndham in 1657.

Entrance to the church is through the S. porch doorway which is particularly fine, its carved spandrels bearing leaf decoration, and within the porch there are two stone chamfered-top benches. In the medieval period, church porches were often places where secular business, particularly legal transactions, took place; the niche, with the figure of the Saint to whom the church was dedicated, being loosely used as an altar, where binding contracts could be sworn. Local courts were held in church porches until the nineteenth century in Alrewas and Yoxall in Staffordshire.

On entering the church nave, the first sight to greet the visitor is the totally unmissable white and grey marble memorial, on the N. wall, to Sir Hugh Wyndham who died in 1684. The monument, carved by John Nost and erected in 1692, is the earliest known example of his work. The impressive Digby Monument in Sherborne Abbey is also by Nost. Originally sited in the chancel the memorial is quite overwhelming, in its size and theatrical presentation, in such a small church. Sir Hugh, in judges' garments (he had been Justice of the Common Pleas) stands centre stage surrounded by a proscenium arch, drapery and two beautifully worked barley-sugar columns. Stage left and right, as it were, kneel his first two, weeping, hour-glass and skull carrying wives who had pre-deceased him. It is, nevertheless, a very fine and elegant memorial, brilliantly carved.

The S. arcade of the nave is late-twelfth-century. The chancel, of the Perp. period, was largely rebuilt in the fifteenth century. The N. chapel, W. tower, S. aisle and S. porch are fifteenth or early-sixteenth-century. The church was restored in 1869–70. The N. chapel, formerly a chantry and currently used as a vestry, has a stone fan-vaulted roof; the corbels, from which the ribs spring, show angels bearing shields.

The interior was decorated, including stained-glass, as part of the restorations of 1869–70, by the ecclesiastical furnishers, Clayton and Bell who also crafted the splendid polychrome reredos above the main altar. The colouring and figure stylisation in the window on the

N. side of the chancel – with the texts, *Who is my neighbour?* and, *For such is the Kingdom of God* – indicates that it is possibly by Clayton and Bell or by Heaton, Butler and Bayne. Alfred Bell came from Silton and some of the glass was a gift from him. In the SW corner of the S. aisle is a window dedicated to the memory of Leah Bell from her husband Alfred. The surrounding border carries a bell rebus – a pictorial pun on the name Bell. Alfred Bell (1832–1895) was a precocious child and his talent for drawing was encouraged by the rector, an amateur artist, Revd H Martin. Bell became a pupil of the architect George Gilbert Scott. John Richard Clayton (1827–1913), was taught drawing by his talented mother, Selina, the daughter of F T Hollingsworth the portrait painter. During the years 1848–9 Clayton studied drawing at a life-school in London and in 1849 he entered the Royal Academy Schools. Clayton and Bell became partners in 1855 and the company which they formed eventually became one of the most prominent ecclesiastical furnishers during the High-Victorian period, employing a number of stained-glass artists who later became famous in their own right. *(See W F Dixon, Bruton and C E Kempe, Donhead St Mary.)* You will either enjoy or not their Victorian stencilled enrichments (which cannot be ignored) in the chancel, the wagon roof and walls of the nave and the S. porch. When the interior lights are switched on the motifs glow richly.

There are numerous fine memorials and well-crafted furnishings in St Nicholas' church including the Creed and Paternoster panels on the E. wall of the chancel which are *c.*early-eighteenth-century.

STOURTON

– South-West Wiltshire

*West of the B3092 Gillingham to
Maiden Bradley road.
O.S.Landranger 183.*

Dedicated to
Saint Peter

Stourhead Garden lies within the parish of Stourton. It is a wonderful and magical place, much loved by many visitors. It is just beyond the Garden that the River Stour rises, at Six Wells Bottom, emerging into the sunlight following its subterranean coursings, occasionally mystically bubbling up, its gentle lyric barely audible, irrigating the earth as it begins its journey to the sea. The Garden was created by Henry Hoare (1705–85), known as 'The Magnificent', a family nickname due to the fact that there were so many Henries. Mystery and imagination, fact and legend, jostle for supremacy.

Alfred the Great was a major figure in this ancient Kingdom of Wessex, confirmed by villages which lay claim to his presence. He, reputedly, prayed at Brixton Deverill on the eve of battle before sallying forth against the Danes at Edington, or here near Stourhead where, allegedly, Alfred raised his standard before marching out to meet the Danish King Guthrum at the same place in AD878. Stourhead's claim is marked by the erection of a lofty tower by Henry Hoare – Alfred's Tower. Wherever, the tales are all part of that magical weave of folklore relating to archetypal, powerful figures which rise out of the landscape; romantic and larger than life, real or legendary. But then, this portion of south-west Wiltshire, north Dorset and east Somerset is also an other-worldly landscape. Bourton is where the three counties meet. In the ancient world boundaries were supernatural places. In one direction it is the domain of mystical

Glastonbury, the Vale of Avalon, legendary Cadbury, Joseph of Arimathea and King Arthur; Stonehenge, with its ancient monoliths, solstices, and attempts to harmonize with a divine power, in another direction; whilst to the south a connection with the Knights Templar and the Crusades. *(See Templecombe.)* These are elements of myth and solid historical fact, possible and impossible, fictitious and true, which have held in thrall the imaginations of generations down the bloody and destructive centuries. It is a beautiful England, where the likes of the fabled King Arthur, or more verifiable kings, trod. It is an ancient England whose landscape, sentiments and ideals Mallory and Tennyson sought to capture in literature.

Stourton *was* the Stourton family, from Saxon times. A Botolph de la Stourton married a daughter of Godwin, first Earl of the West Saxons, and it was his son who built Stourton House. It was sometimes called Stourton Castle and is still referred to, locally, by that name due in part to oral transmission and also, possibly, to John Leland, the antiquary, having described it in the mid-sixteenth century as, '… embatelid castelle lyke.' After generations of historically gripping, rising and plunging family fortunes the Stourton main line finally expired in Parisian exile in 1720. The Stourtons supported Henry VIII in ending Roman Catholicism in England, despite being Roman Catholic themselves; consequently they benefited greatly from the Dissolution of the Monasteries. However, following an initial glow of hubristic satisfaction, a steady nemesis of decline ensued, starting with William, seventh Lord Stourton, who had been given the Manor of Kilmington, the tenant of which was a William Hartgill, who held the Manor from the Monastery. A most bitter feud developed and the Hartgills, father and son, were murdered by Charles, eighth Lord Stourton; a deed for which he was hanged in 1557. *(For a fuller account of this episode see Kilmington.)* The end came with Edward, thirteenth Lord Stourton, who died, exiled in Paris, intestate and childless. The heavily mortgaged estate was taken over for three years by Sir Thomas Meres in 1714. It is very likely that the property was in a very parlous condition having been sacked by Edmund Ludlow *(see Longbridge Deverill)* and his Parliamentarians in 1644.

Richard Hoare (1648–1718), Lord Mayor of London in 1712, founded Hoare's Bank in 1672 under the sign of The Golden Bottle in Cheapside, London. The Bank, now in Fleet Street, still exists, under the name of C Hoare & Co., as an independant private bank. His son Henry Hoare (1677–1725) bought the Manor of Stourton in 1717 and engaged Colen Campbell to design a new building for him. Stourton was demolished in 1717 and Stourhead was built between 1721–5. Further additions were made later.

Stourhead is now a National Trust property, having been gifted to them by the Hoare family in 1946. It was a most fortunate acquisition. The entire ensemble arrangement of buildings and gardens harmonize superbly, from the elegant archway and tree-lined approach to Stourhead House, the Spread Eagle Inn and its surrounding buildings, to the famous gardens, at the entrance of which is the beautiful Bristol High Cross, largely dating from 1373. It stands on its own, slightly elevated, turf mound opposite Stourton village church of St Peter. The whole is so neat, clean and tidy, as ordered by the National Trust, that the visitor may wonder if the manicured lawns and verges in the village centre are vacuum cleaned prior to their arrival.

St Peter's church is not a National Trust property (neither is the Spread Eagle Inn). It is a living church, not redundant or a museum, and is not supported by the Trust. However it is, in an historical sense, in the joint ownership of the Stourtons and the Hoares; their deathly presence in the building being in close proximity to each other.

The church is a small compact building in its own picturesque setting. It is in a Late-Perp. style, and, due to it being largely of one period, is of a fairly unified appearance. The architecturally plain W. tower has a simply embattled top but no W. door, it having been sealed at sometime during the nineteenth century. In the fifteenth century four sets of three-light clerestory windows glazed in clear white glass were added on either side of the nave. One of the few refinements to the building is in the attractive parapets, comprised of cusped lozenges and triangles, added during the lifetime of Sir Richard Colt Hoare (1758–1838). However trim and well maintained now, in 1553 St Peter's was declared to be in a ruinous condition.

This state of affairs corresponded with the period of Charles, eighth Lord Stourton, murderer of William and John Hartgill.

Internally there are arcades of four bays to N. and S. which are possibly of the thirteenth century as the line of a thirteenth-century building can easily be followed in the church. The S. aisle was added in 1848 to provide more seating. In the N. aisle is a Late-Norman font which came from the redundant church of St Alfred the Great, Monkton Deverill, beneath which lies the Stourton family vault.

There is little stained-glass in St Peter's but in the N. aisle is a window half-glazed in white glass whilst the upper half has remains, badly faded, of what is probably fifteenth-century figurative glass. The other two windows dated 1859 are by David Evans (1793–1861), who was a partner of John Betton of Shrewsbury. On Betton's retirement in 1825, Evans took over the company.

The chancel was refurbished during the Victorian period. Dividing the nave from chancel stood a rood screen and loft which was removed by one of the Henry Hoares, possibly Henry Ainslie Hoare (1824–94). The present altar in the sanctuary, which replaced the Victorian altar and reredos, is from 1937. The E. window was also blocked off but the glazed window is still in situ and can be seen from the outside. Why was this effected?

St Peter's is rich in monuments relating to the Stourtons and the Hoares, particularly the latter. One of the most prominent monuments is the large tomb-chest at the E. end of the N. aisle, which is to Edward, sixth Lord Stourton (d.1636) and his wife Agnes. The two recumbent figures are in prayerful attitude, with three kneeling, very small scale, children at their head; he armoured, she simply but attractively dressed. It was the sixth Lord Stourton who supported HenryVIII in his wilful destruction of the monasteries. The figures and tomb, ironically, bear the usual signs of desecratory damage.

The Hoare family memorials are in the S. aisle. That of Henry Hoare (dated 1724) one time MP for the City of London and the builder of Stourhead, is on the E. wall of the S. aisle. It is tall and elegant with a number of architectural refinements; a Classical tympanum or pediment having a portrait bust of Henry Hoare within the open apex, Corinthian capitalled columns and two flaming Grecian urns to left and right. On the S. wall of the S. aisle is a memorial to Henry Hoare, 'The Magnificent' (d.1785), who laid out the gardens. It is surmounted by two large well-fed putti supporting a large garlanded urn. Still on the S. wall but moving W. is a memorial tablet to Henry Peregrine Rennie Hoare who died in 1981. Moving still further W. towards the corner is a very elegant memorial, sculpted in Italy, to Hester Colt Hoare (d.1785). It is of white marble with a pink granite faux sarcophagus in the upper section, above which is a black granite urn supported by two small putti. In the lower section of this memorial is a tablet to Sir Richard Colt Hoare (d.1838) builder of the library and picture gallery in Stourhead House. Moving eastwards there is an alcove, separated from the nave by a low screen, containing a fireplace. It is probably what was known as a parlour pew. Originally it could have been a small chantry chapel; there are a number of churches where such a change has taken place. In the alcove is a wall tablet to Sir Henry Hugh Arthur Hoare (d.1947) and his wife, Alda, who died later the same day. It was they who gave Stourhead to the National Trust.

In the churchyard, to the SE of the chancel, is a mausoleum, which is largely of two styles, the sarcophagus Classical and the canopy Gothic, where members of the Hoare family are buried, including Sir Richard Colt Hoare. It was made during the lifetime of that culturally attractive, physically elegant and academically capable man.

Within the compass of Stourton, Stourhead House and Gardens and, St Peter's Church, there is a wealth of beauty and culture. It is hardly surprising, therefore, that Stourhead is one of the most visited National Trust houses in England.

STURMINSTER NEWTON
– North Dorset

On the B3092. South of Gillingham, south-west of Shaftesbury.
O.S.Landranger 194.

Dedicated to Saint Mary

Sturminster Newton, traditional
capital of the Blackmore Vale,
the 'Stourcastle' of Thomas
Hardy, is a small well-hidden ancient market town of a quite
distinctive character. The Blackmore Vale, Hardy's 'vale of the little
dairies', is a large area of outstanding beauty; still very rural, still
lushly agricultural. If you have a fancy for the bustle of a country
town of robust character then Monday, market day in 'Stur', is the
day to visit.

Sturminster – the first part of the name derives from the river, the
Stour, which runs through the town but 'minster' is more puzzling.
The church notes explain, 'In Dorset we have a number of minsters:
apart from the two on the banks of the Stour (our own and Sturminster
Marshall), there come to mind Beaminster, Charminster, Yetminster,
Wimborne Minster, Iwerne Minster and Lychett Minster.' What then
is a minster? Minster churches were served by a group of priests,
their ministry spread over a large territory; they were churches
attached to a monastery – in this case Glastonbury.

The very active church of St Mary lies very quietly detached, but
certainly not aloof, on the south side of the tightly-packed buildings
in the town centre and is easily reached on foot. There are a number
of interesting buildings surrounding the church. An area known as
Tanyard explains what went on there, and the house possessing that
name most likely dates to *c*.1300 and is the oldest inhabited dwelling
place in the town. On the east side of the church, adjacent to the
boundary wall, is The Old School House, a handsome building,
which, it is believed, the young William Barnes, the Dorset dialect
poet and cleric, attended.

St Mary's is described by Sir Nicholas Pevsner as, '... a strange building, big and serious.' It *is* large but the size becomes more obvious from within. The nave, W. tower and N. and S. aisles are late-fourteenth or early-fifteenth-century. As the church notes point out, '... if you sit in the front pew of the nave, everything you see to right, left and front, was rebuilt in 1825'.

Thomas Henry Lane Fox *(see Tollard Royal)* became curate at St Mary's in 1824, when the vicar was Revd James Michael. Lane Fox was socially well-placed in polite society; his father was a major landowner in Yorkshire and his mother, a sister to the lord of the manor, George Pitt. The church notes state that the lord of the manor had the power to appoint the vicar, therefore, it was a foregone conclusion that when Thomas Henry was appointed curate he would, eventually, become vicar; which he did fifteen years later. It has been estimated that even as the youngest son he had a personal fortune of around £100,000 (in old money). Knowing that he would eventually become vicar of St Mary's, Thomas Henry, almost immediately after he had been appointed curate, had the building surveyed and engaged an architect to draw up plans for a new building; all of that, in fact, which can be seen right, left and front from the front pew. On 28 April 1825 the foundation stone, which can be seen on the exterior E. wall of the chancel, was laid and the entire project completed on 20 March 1828. Additionally, he provided new pews throughout the church, donated a new organ and erected iron railings around the boundary of the building which, the visitor will observe, are no longer in-situ, only the stubby evidence of where they, no doubt, once elegantly stood. They most likely disappeared just after the outbreak of WWII when Lord Beaverbrook the then proprietor of the *Daily Express* newspaper had the crackpot idea of denuding the entire nation of its railings to help the war effort by melting them down and transforming them into guns, aeroplanes, tanks etc. The entire scheme, playing on British patriotism, ended up with the railings being dumped somewhere at the bottom of the North Sea. When you see burned-off railings, thank Lord Beaverbrook. The only railings left could be heard from all those people who had lost theirs!

It is known from records kept by a former churchwarden and local solicitor, Thomas Dashwood, that the cost of the entire restoration amounted to around £40,000 (old money). When the remarkable Revd Lane Fox died in November 1861 his financial assets amounted to £2-19s-5d; as the church notes observe, '... his whole fortune having been spent on his parishioners.'

The W. tower is comprised of four stages, separated by plain string-coursing. The first stage has diagonal buttressing rising to the first string-course and bears the trefoil-headed two-light W. window. At the second stage there is a repeat W. window uniform with the first stage. The bell-openings with trefoil piercings are at the third stage immediately below the clock faces. An interesting lattice-panelled stage is situated directly below the nineteenth-century embattled parapet, with its large crocketted corner-pinnacles and smaller pinnacles centred between the corners. The entire church is built of ashlar blocks of Shaftesbury greensand. The tower carries a ring of six bells; the tenor by John Wallis (*see Fifehead Magdalen*) (inscribed 1612) is the oldest, the second (originally 1625) was recast in 1862 and the rest are from 1827. Entrance is through the W. door.

What was the internal W. arch of the tower, has now been attractively and successfully remodelled by the filling-in of the entire arch with a wood and glass structure. It provides a sort of air-lock between the outer W. door and the inner W. door. Previously the bell-sallies hung down into the entrance, there being no separate ringing chamber. This untidiness has now been overcome by the creation of a floor, providing a bell-ringing platform; result – a team of contented campanologists! (However, the effect of the very important *Nativity* W. window is rather lost. Under the old arrangement, the window could easily be seen from the nave, but now it can only be observed through the large glass window of the ringing-chamber.) The interior is high, light and very airy with a clear-glass clerestory, above which is a superb wagon roof with flying angels *c.*late-fifteenth/early-sixteenth-centuries.

Of all of the churches explored in this work, St Mary's, Sturminster has some of the finest examples of stained and painted glass. Some of the windows are truly outstanding works of ecclesiastical art and for the connoisseur of church glass it would be well worth the pilgrimage to Sturminster. For the most part the large windows are of plain white lozenge, or diaper-shaped, glass making those which are stained and painted leap out at the viewer.

There are two windows by Mary Lowndes (1857–1929). Her father, Canon Richard Lowndes, was rector here when the W. tower underwent a restoration in 1884. He was faced with a dilemma; professional and familial; he could either allow his daughter's window of *The Nativity* (created as a memorial to her mother) to be placed in a prominent position in his church and stand being accused of nepotism (as the comprehensive church leaflet on Mary Lowndes by Nancy Armstrong FRSA points out) or place it in a less prominent position and disappoint his daughter. He chose the latter option and her first ever church window was placed in the tower. However, nothing can take away Mary Lowndes' achievement of being the first notable female stained-glass artist to permanently display her work and take her place in church stained-glass history.

Martin Harrison in *Victorian Stained Glass*, citing, *The Art Journal* for 1896 tells us, 'Miss Lowndes worked for some little time with Henry Holiday *[see Mere]* at cartoon making but as regards the technique of glass painting she is self-taught. Mr. Christopher Whall *[see Maiden Bradley]* has not been without influence upon Miss Lowndes and she speaks with the enthusiasm of a pupil about him. Miss Lowndes relies upon her drawing from the model in her cartoons, but as the actual glass painting is done by her the necessity of making elaborate cartoons does not exist.' What *The Art Journal* does not say is that Mary had been a student of the Slade School of Art (part of University College, London) from 1883 before becoming a pupil of Henry Holiday. A company called Britten and Gilson had developed an 'Early English' glass in 1889 for the Arts and Crafts architect Edward Schroeder Prior (1852–1932). The glass, named slab glass, was thick and uneven which encouraged an emphasis on colour and texture and discouraged artists from overpainting their work. Those artists, including Mary, who wished to use the slab glass made for Prior had to have their windows made by Britten and Gilson, who were then in Southwark Street,

London and in fact that is where her *Nativity* window was made. In 1897 she joined with Alfred John Drury (1868–1940) who had previously been a foreman at Britten and Gilson and the pair went into partnership under the name of Lowndes and Drury, taking premises at 35, Park Walk, Chelsea but in 1906 they opened a new workshop which they named The Glass House, at Lettice Street, Fulham.

Mary also worked with Isobel Lilian Gloag, (1865–1917) a painter and illustrator. The S. window in the Warrior Chapel, inspired by the Arts-and-Crafts-Movement, dedicated to her father who died in 1898, was made in collaboration with Isobel in 1901. It is in total contrast to the *Nativity* window. Its theme, spread over three lights, is the Resurrection. Mary designed many windows, not all with religious themes; it is estimated that she made over one hundred in total. But of her windows in St Mary's, Nancy Armstrong says, 'These two windows by her, are possibly the most vulnerable, personal and interesting of all.'

The large E. window of *Christ in Majesty*, a typical Victorian work, bright and arresting, is by John Hardman & Co.Ltd. John Hardman (1811–1867) was originally a worker in metal and through a friendship with A W N Pugin he made the hands and numerals for the clock face of the Big Ben tower at the Palace of Westminster. It was also Pugin who suggested to Hardman that he should expand into stained-glass, which he did and became one of the pioneers of the revival of stained glass in the Victorian period. Hardman founded the company in 1838, initially selling church furnishings and fittings and branched out in 1845 by opening a stained-glass department at Paradise Street, Birmingham. The company eventually became John Hardman & Co. Ltd., operating from 43, Newhall Hill, Birmingham with London premises at 1, Albemarle Street, W1. The E. window of Worcester Cathedral is also by Hardman.

In the N. transept, W. wall is a window dedicated to Selena Davis and Mary Dashwood, designed by Alexander Gibbs, (1832–1886) the second of seven sons, of whom three became artists in stained-glass. After forming a partnership with his brother Isaac they parted company in 1885 and from then on worked independently.

Alexander's premises were at 38, Bloomsbury Square, London WC1 from 1858 to 1875 and it is this address which is recorded on the window, bottom right-hand light.

The N. aisle window of the *Crucifixion* was dedicated in 1911 to Evan M Mansell-Pleydell RHA, who died at Lucknow 22 May 1910 aged twenty-five, and to his twin brother, John who died 22 September 1916 at Amiens during the Battle of the Somme. The window was designed by Geoffrey Fuller Webb (1879–1954) of East Grinstead. Webb trained with C E Kempe *(see Donhead St Mary)* and Ninian Comper *(see Whitham Friary)*. In its overall design and palette one can detect the influence of the latter. The window is signed with one of Webb's characteristic glass marks – a spider's web.

The three-light window in the S. aisle by Harry Clarke (1889–1931) is the *ne plus ultra* of stained-glass windows.

Harry Clarke worked in his father's studio J Clarke & Sons in Dublin at 6, 7 and 33, Frederick Street, which was founded in 1886 and eventually closed in 1973. As a student he attended the Royal College of Art, London and the Dublin School of Art. In 1921 (the year of this window) he and his brother took over their father's studio. From 1925 he appears to have worked at Lowndes and Drury's The Glass House, (during the latter years of Mary Lowndes' life – she died in 1929). The window is dedicated to Roma Spencer-Smith, wife of Sir Drummond Spencer-Smith and to their son Sir Thomas Spencer-Smith.

It is worth journeying to Sturminster *solely* for the purpose of seeing this work of art which is, quite simply, awe-inspiring; the faces of the figures are haunting. The constantly moving natural light from outside passes through the scintillating jewels of slab glass, of the most saturated colours. Martin Harrison in *Victorian Stained Glass*, is perfectly correct when describing Harry Clarke's work in general as being in the, '… Pre-Raphaelite tradition …', with a '… Beardsley-esque decadence …' and a '… Byzantine dignity …'. In the centre light there is a depiction of the Madonna and Child; in the left light, Elizabeth of Hungary (patron saint of nurses) and in the right, St Barbara (patron saint of artillerymen and miners). *(See Cucklington for further reference to St Barbara.)*

Clarke's attention to the minutest of detail is masterly. Once the viewer has recovered from the effect of the whole window, it is suggested that they concentrate on one feature at a time: for example, the footwear on the figures. They cease to be merely painted-on-glass shoes; they are so brilliantly executed that the viewer can identify the material from which they are meant to be made!

There is a plethora of memorial wall-plaques and floor-slabs throughout the church, but the one on the E. wall of the N. transept is possibly the most memorable and elegant. It is dedicated to Sir Owen Morshead 1893–1977 G.C.V.O., K.C.B., D.S.O., M.C., Fellow of Magdalene College, Cambridge and Librarian of Windsor Castle for thirty-two years. The memorial is also dedicated to his wife Paquita 1905–2002.

There are three, particularly excellently-carved, screens. The chancel screen has a large and simple unadorned rood on the cross-member. The N. transept screen, which separates the vestry and organ from the crossing, is dedicated to Henry Charles and Emma Dashwood. It has a carved Gothic tracery top and a linen-fold decorated panel below; a brilliantly sustained piece of carving worked over a large area. The carved screen in the S. chancel aisle separates off the Warrior Chapel from the transept. This chapel is dedicated to the memory of the men of Sturminster Newton who died during WWI and WWII.

There are two further fine wooden furnishings: one, the oak seating in the choir; the other, the noble carved lectern, a joyous outburst of artistic affection, which commemorates William Barnes, the Dorset poet, scholar and cleric. Both were created by William Westcott, a chorister here for forty years.

The county of Dorset has witnessed the genesis of two outstanding writers: Thomas Hardy (1840–1928) and William Barnes (1801–1886). The one achieving an international literary fame, the other remaining largely parochial.

Barnes, although born at Bagber which is about two miles west of the town, was a child of Sturminster Newton who played around the town's broken market cross as a small boy. He was educated at the small Dames' School and attended St Mary's church.

When Barnes was aged thirteen a local lawyer (and churchwarden) Thomas Henry Dashwood, enquired of the local headmaster whether a boy might be found who could write in a decent hand and Barnes was sent to see him. As a result Barnes left school at fourteen to work in his office. Following Dashwood's death, Barnes moved to Dorchester to fulfil a similar clerical role. Like many boys of humble background but with a solid fundamental education, Barnes had a genius at his back to drive him forward, with much to learn and prove to himself and the world; driven youth does not lie idle. In both Sturminster and Dorchester his employers, and the clergy of those towns, helped further his education by teaching him Latin and Greek, extending his artistic ability and encouraging his musical talents.

In 1820 his first poems were published, followed in 1822 by *Orra, a Lapland Tale*. In 1823 he left Dorchester for Mere in Wiltshire, *(see Mere)* to take over a small school. Barnes married Julia Miles in 1827 whom he had first met in Dorchester. They expanded the school into one for boarders and remained in Mere until 1835 which were years of intense happiness; full of learning, teaching and writing. The Barnes' moved back to Dorchester and founded another boarding school for the specific purpose of educating middle-class boys for entry into the universities, the professions, the army and the navy.

In 1837 he enrolled as a 'ten-year man' at St John's College, Cambridge, a major undertaking involving periods of residence, for a course of study leading ultimately to a Bachelor of Divinity degree. Barnes was ordained deacon at Salisbury Cathedral in 1847, becoming priest in 1848 and in the same year was appointed curate at Whitcombe, near Dorchester. He was awarded his degree in 1850. Following the death of Julia in 1852 their school in Dorchester gradually declined throughout the rest of the decade. Trevor Hearl, the author of *William Barnes: The Schoolmaster*, quoted by Chris Wrigley in *William Barnes the Dorset Poet*, wrote, 'In the year of the Great Exhibition, the Rev. William Barnes' Academy was one of the largest, and potentially best-equipped, schools in Dorset for the sons of the middle classes.' In 1861, financial security for Barnes was achieved through the grant of a small literary pension, amounting to £30 per annum, from Queen Victoria on Lord Palmerston's recommendation, for his dialect poetry and he was offered the parish of Winterborne Came, just outside Dorchester, where he remained for the rest of his life.

Barnes, writing of his poems, *Rural Life in the Dorset Dialect*, published in 1844, hoped, '... that if this little work should fall into the hands of a reader of that class in whose language it is written, it would not be likely to damp his love of God or hurt the tone of his moral sentiments, or the dignity of his self-respect ... not to show up the simplicity of rural life as an object of sport ...'

Although he may not have returned to live in the area where he was born and spent his childhood, he never left it either, his entire corpus of dialect poetry, (there were more in 1859 and 1862) is imbued with his rural background. The dialect poems are not mere conceits (as Barnes himself indicated above) full of sentimental quaintness – for he was a serious scholar – they are his lyric songs of 'innocence and experience'; profound and witty. Barnes' poetry is simple, sincere and quintessentially English in its character where he describes a picture of life and work in rural England. He had also developed other intellectual passions, for example philology, and was the possessor of a sensitive musical ear, not only for music itself but for languages and for the verse forms of Welsh, Irish, Anglo-Saxon, Persian and Hebraic.

Barnes' writings of rural life and work followed a long well-worn path first trodden by the Greek poets Hesiod (*floruit c.*BC700), Theocritus (*c.*BC300–*c.*260) and, that great poet of the Augustan Golden Age of Latin poetry, Virgil (BC70–19) through his *Eclogues* (a word Barnes also used) and his *Georgics*. He has much in common with John Clare, (1793–1864) a major talent and another long-neglected rural genius. Of more modern writers, it should be said that whatever the fame of Hardy's writing, poetry and prose, there is a golden thread running through his work, which Hardy himself recognised, linking it to Barnes. Barnes' influence also runs through the sensuous and ascetic poetry of the Jesuit poet Gerard Manley Hopkins (1844–1889). Barnes, himself and his work, also influenced another Sturminster Newton writer Robert Young (1811–1908), who became a friend and followed him in the writing of dialect verse.

Barnes' dialect verse is not easy, it requires patience and application by the reader and a will to engage with it. W H Auden wrote of him, 'I cannot enjoy one poem by Shelley and am delighted by every line by William Barnes.' Those of a certain age of maturity will recall from their golden youth the school choir singing *Linden Lea*, set to the music of Ralph Vaughan Williams.

Within the woodlands, flowery gladed,
By the oak tree's mossy root,
The shining grass-blades, timber-shaded,
Now do quiver underfoot;
And birds do whistle overhead,
And water's bubbling in its bed,
And there for me the apple tree
Do lean down low in Linden Lea.

Its full title is *My Orcha'd in Linden Lea*. It was one of Barnes' dialect poems and for the purpose of it being nationally understood was taken out of its Dorset context.

'Ithin the woodlands, flow'ry gleäded,
By the woak tree's mossy moot,
The sheenen grass-bleädes, timber-sheäded,
Now do quiver under voot;
An' birds do whissle over head,
An' water's bubblen in its bed,
An' there vor me the apple tree
Do leän down low in Linden Lea.

The influence of the church on Barnes' life was enormous, his Christian faith is directly reflected throughout his writings during his long life.

SUTTON WALDRON
– North Dorset

*South of Shaftesbury. On the A350 Shaftesbury
to Blandford section. O.S.Landranger 183.*

Dedicated to Saint Bartholomew

Halfway between Shaftesbury and
Blandford is a church not to be
missed. A Victorian Gothic Revival
building described by Sir John
Betjeman in his *Parish Churches of
England and Wales* as, 'The *beau idéal*
of mid-Victorian romanticism, one
of the prettiest churches in the
county.' It is easy to find, with ample
parking at the end of the lane where it is sited. The first things to note
are the ornate cast-iron Victorian railings and double gates; a credit
to the making of casting iron into an art form. The carved stone gate
pillars are equally superb; a welcome beginning to a visit.

The church replaced a Saxon building, not quite on the same site,
but on slightly higher ground. In 1884 Canon Anthony Huxtable was
appointed rector, '… a man of tremendous energy and drive', to
quote the church notes. The Saxon church was in a terrible state
possibly from rising damp, as this creeping menace afflicts and also
affects the present St Bartholomew's, and by 1834 the church was
also too small for the expanding population. Canon Huxtable, being
the driving force he obviously was, filled with enthusiasm (a word
which is incidentally taken from the Greek *enthousiasmos* – 'to be
filled with the God') for matters ecclesiastical, demolished the old
building and, at his own and his wife's expense, erected the new one.
Additionally, the Canon was passionately interested in the
development of agriculture, as he was directly engaged himself in
matters agrarian. He encouraged his farming parishioners to adopt
his own methods of husbandry for themselves.

St Bartholomew's is completely a Victorian Gothic Revival church with nothing residual from its Saxon ancestor (apart from a few oddments of fourteenth-century stonework, noted by the RCHM report following their visit in the early 1970s) and no architectural carbuncle grafted on at a later date. Externally and internally it is a beautiful period piece in a lovely rural setting. It is built from Marnhull and Mapperton stone, which in the passing one hundred and fifty-odd years has taken on a fascinating patina, particularly the W. tower with diagonal corner buttressing. The tower is partly rendered and partly smooth-faced ashlar blocks. The nave, chancel and sacristy are of flint and squared-off rubble blocks. The red scalloped-edged roof-tiles are in excellent condition.

Augustus Welby Northmore Pugin (1812–1852), who worked with Sir Charles Barry on the Houses of Parliament, published two seminal architectural works: in 1836, *Contrasts; or a Parallel Between the Architecture of the 15th and 19th Centuries* and in 1841 *True Principles of Christian Architecture*. Both had a profound effect upon Victorian architectural thinking; the result was a Gothic revival. The church here was designed by George Alexander (d.1883) and consecrated in 1847. (Alexander also designed the Romanesque church at East Stour in 1842, St John, Enmore Green in 1843 and St Mary, Motcombe in 1846.)

There are a number of architectural refinements to the tower; the embellished octagonal spire, built entirely from ashlar blocks, does not soar but is, nevertheless, a very prominent landmark for some distance around. The crocketed corner pinnacles of the tower rise from the corner buttressing, each one graced with its own elegant finial and each, in turn, providing support for the equally elegant flying-buttresses, fretted with trefoil tracery. A fine touch is the embrasured mural crown placed like a collar at the base of the broached spire and passing beneath each flying-buttress; the whole resting delicately above the carved gargoyled string-course. The W. window of the tower is comprised of four ogee-headed lights with geometrical tracery. Alexander's design is Decorated period Gothic, which became known to architects as 'second-pointed' (Early-English period – 'first-pointed'; Perpendicular period – 'third-pointed'). Decorated period forms were aesthetically discerned as the most perfect of the three periods.

On entering through the S. porch the first furnishing the visitor will see is the impressive font and cover. The traditional arrangement of a font at the W. end of a church symbolises the beginning of the Christian journey ultimately leading to the altar and to God. This font is octagonal with stencilled biblical texts below the moulded rim; the elaborate, oak pyramidal cover has no fill-in panels but open sides, the angles being crocketed. The entire ensemble is placed on a splendid Victorian tiled raised platform. From 1236 font covers became compulsory in England. Traditionally the font water was blessed on Easter Sunday and allowed to remain in its receptacle for a long period, which explains why fonts are of stone, because of its general lack of porosity, and why in some there are lead linings. Once blessed, the Holy Water had to be protected from dirt and, importantly, from being stolen for its perceived magical properties, to prevent its use in charms and ritualistic acts.

St Bartholomew's is constantly beset by damp and by the early 1980s the building was in a very parlous condition. In addition to the damp, the roof was leaking and broken guttering had caused considerable damage. However, cometh the hour, cometh the man; that man was Peter Baillie. Distressed and, no doubt, disgusted at what had happened to his much loved church he set out to research its architectural and internal decorative background. As interesting as that was it was insufficient, as actual restoration was desperately required, so he led like-minded others on a quest for funds to enable them to carry out the work. As if nature and the lack of maintenance alone had not caused sufficient havoc on the fabric, an enormous and mindless act of vandalism had been visited upon the interior in the 1950s by an almost complete overpainting of the original colour scheme, apart from the ceiling, at a time when things Victorian were becoming totally unfashionable. Much fine Victorian work in many spheres was deliberately destroyed in the 1950s and 1960s. It was the beginning of the age of architectural brutalism. Victoriana had to be expunged. Much of this was founded on guilt-ridden angst relating to our British imperial, colonial past and gravely insulted the Victorian genius. According to the church notes, even as late as 1978, it was proposed that the whole interior should be whitewashed!

The original internal colour scheme was designed by Owen Jones (1809–1874), who is often referred to as a colour theorist but he was also an architect and ornamental designer. Jones had a great influence on the use of iron and colour in buildings. He was appointed Superintendent of Works for the Great Exhibition in 1851 and responsible for the decoration of Joseph Paxton's Crystal Palace. When the Crystal Palace was re-erected at Sydenham, Jones designed the Egyptian and Alhambra Courts his knowledge based, it would appear, on his extensive travels around the Mediterranean from the 1830s.

Restoration work on Owen Jones scheme of decoration began in 1982; it was then when the original beauty began to surface. The walls had been painted a cool lavender-blue, bordered by lettered biblical texts. The chancel had been enriched with stencilled patterns, gilding, lettering and a wonderful red and blue colour theme. Repair and consolidation of the plaster and paint was undertaken to help recreate the harmonies of colour sought by Owen Jones. New gold-leaf was applied to the damaged areas around the chancel for example, and suitably toned down to match the original colour. The plaster repairs were carried out by professional restorers Donald and Rachael Smith. The repairs and restorations, apart from the internal tower, were completed in 1994. Unfortunately, due to the ravages of damp, further repairs have been necessary since that date. The tower project began in 1999 with external work and internal plastering and redecoration. In the tower there are two bells by Mears (a company now incorporated into the Whitechapel Bell Foundry), which have been recast, a replacement for an unsafe bell-frame installed and the bell-chamber floor replaced; all of which has cost around £15,000. The total amount of expenditure since 1982 is some £200,000, met by the parishioners, fund-raising events and a generous grant from English Heritage. The Parochial Church Council, appropriately, asks the visitor to make a contribution towards the maintenance of this now largely restored building; it well deserves it.

The stone polychromatic square pulpit is, quite simply, beautiful. On its front is a carved Lamb and Flag emblem in a recessed roundel and on the side a further roundel with a large carved Cross Patée. Below the moulded pulpit top are stencilled biblical texts. When facing the altar, the lectern on the right-hand side of the nave is again a glorious affair; stone with a moulded coping above trefoil-headed arcading, resting on elegantly turned shafts. This entire ensemble is decorated in a superbly intense polychromatic style. The high chancel arch and nave arcades are also enhanced by gilded and stencilled decoration.

The chancel communion rails are also of stone with moulded top and bottom – trefoil tracery separating the two. The wooden centre gate is similarly styled; the whole in a polychromatic finish. In the chancel is a stone sedilia and on the N. side a small niche with an ogee head. Arching over all is the outstanding chancel ceiling with polychromatic beams and blue painted panels, the field of each filled with gilded stars; a scintilating compostella. Whilst the visitor is looking upwards at the night sky, underfoot, in both chancel and nave, are geometrical patterned encaustic floor-tiles, *(see Upton Noble)* reputedly designed by the great A W N Pugin himself.

Behind the altar is a carved stone reredos inset with four panels, each panel filled with a carved traditional symbolic representation of one of the four evangelists. The E. window, a beautifully executed example of stained and painted glass, is in a deliberately archaizing style of the fourteenth century which, according to the RCHM report of 1972, is by Hudson and Powell (a company of which, in my record, no trace can be found).

The nave pews are of unusual configuration; eye-catching and attractive. Forget any ideas of typical Victorian pews with upright solid bench ends. Even the original pew numbers are still attached to the bench uprights; now out of sequence due to the pews having been moved around.

Allowing for past and ongoing problems relating to dampness, the church is a fine manifestation of Victorian ecclesiological thinking based on Gothic Revival concepts. In all its colourfulness, its biblical texts and the bold and striking designs of its furnishings, St Bartholomew's is probably something akin to, but possibly more sophisticated than, how a genuine medieval church must have appeared to its worshippers. Only one other exists in England in which Owen Jones, as far as is known, made a similar artistic contribution and that is in the totally different setting of urban Streatham, London. Christ Church is sited at an intensely busy traffic-lighted cross-roads, its floodlit detached campanile a welcome and uplifting beacon on a dark night in south London. St Bartholomew's, Sutton Waldron and Christ Church, Streatham have something in common apart from their fundamental message; they can both be seen by the traveller from some distance.

What a joy it must have been in St Bartholomews on the day the church was consecrated in 1847; to enter and sit quietly, but be internally excited, amidst this architectural gem by George Alexander, to absorb the vibrant colour scheme by Owen Jones and to offer up a prayer of thanksgiving to Canon and Mrs Anthony Huxtable who made it all possible.

Do visit their graves on the N. side, E. end exterior of the chancel before you depart. *Nunc dimittis* and *pax vobiscum*.

❋❋❋

Postscript.
The Builder Journal, issue number 27, dated November 1847, page 565, carried the following report relating to the rebuilding of St Bartholomew's church:

CHURCH BUILDING
The parish church of Sutton Waldron, near Shaftesbury, having been rebuilt, was consecrated on Tuesday, the 16th instant, by the Bishop of Salisbury. … and accommodates 200 to 250 persons. The style adopted is the decorated. …

The total length inside, 80 feet; width, 30 feet; height
of tower and spire, 112 feet. The body of the church is
paved with stone, the whole of the seating being uniform
and moveable. The chancel floor is inlaid with encaustic
tiles by Minton. The windows of the chancel are of
painted glass by Hudson and Powell. … The communion
table is carved in oak; and a gilt eagle-desk stands at the
steps of the chancel. A portion of the west end of the aisle
is devoted to the baptistry, the floor and steps to the font
being of encaustic tiles, and illuminated inscriptions being
written on the walls. The font cover is carved in oak. …
In order to render the whole complete, the rector has
furnished the church with new bells and silver
communion-service, as well as carpets and velvet furniture
to pulpit, desk, etc. The work has been well executed by
Mr.Green of Pimperne, Dorsetshire, *without* a clerk of works,
from the designs of Mr.Alexander.

SWALLOWCLIFFE
– South-West Wiltshire

*On the north side of A30 Shaftesbury
to Wilton road. O.S.Landranger 184.*

Dedicated to Saint Peter

Alec Clifton-Taylor observed
that the south of Wiltshire
yielded few parish churches
of note, apart from Salisbury, Chilmark and Tisbury; Sir John
Betjeman thought the county unlucky in having T H Wyatt, whom
he considered one of the dullest of Victorian architects; whilst
Nicholas Pevsner 'assumed' that George Gilbert Scott, the architect
of St Peter's, ' … did not look back with pleasure' at his neo-Norman
church at Swallowcliffe. St Peter's fits none of those observations.
Here is a church worthy of some note. It is not by Wyatt. There is a
superb harmony in its design, with the odd, but interesting,
dissonant note. It is built of light-coloured stone (possibly from the
local Chilmark quarries), much of it very likely re-used from an
earlier church on the same site. However, as the present edifice is
larger than the previous one, new material was added. The ashlar
blocks are now decoratively weathered, possessing the wonderful
patina of circular patches of lichen.

Those visitors wishing to learn more about the previous church
should consult the excellent church guide, *The Churches of St Peter,
Swallowcliffe, Wiltshire,1976,* by Commander S Jenkins.

The prospect which the visitor first glimpses is one of a seriously
beautiful neo-Norman church, partly framed by foreground trees. St
Peter's is sited somewhat higher than the visitor and with sunlight
flooding the subject and the tall heavily canopied trees providing
deep and sombre shade, a strong dramatic tension is created.

St Peter's (1842–3) was designed by Scott and Moffatt in the neo-
Norman style, it being fashionable around that time. It is also referred
to as Romanesque, Early Christian or Byzantine. Sir George Gilbert

Scott (1811–78) was greatly influenced by A W N Pugin's writings on Medieval architecture and as a result became one of the leading exponents of the Gothic style, highly regarded in the High Victorian period. So much so in fact, that it was Scott who designed the Albert Memorial (1862–3) and St Pancras Station Hotel (1865) and worked on Salisbury, Ely and Litchfield Cathedrals and on Westminster Abbey.

One possibly thinks of original Norman architecture as heavy, however it is not here, as there is an unmistakable lightness of touch in both the exterior and the interior and there are a small number of departures from the neo-Norman style in the windows and stair-turret spirelet. There is striking four-arch arcading in both N. and S. leading through to narrow aisles. The piers on the N. side are round with decorated capitals, whilst those on the S. are octagonal with plain capitals. If you appreciate Romanesque style then there is much to enjoy: the carved stone pulpit and reading desk complement each other beautifully; the simple fretted work of the wooden chancel rails with the altar table which is held aloft on well-proportioned stone shafts and the eyecatching carved stone font which is mounted on a stone drum surrounded by intersected arches resting on stone shafts. The whole, has an aura of grace about it.

The W. window of 1870, a single long light, is dedicated to George Gerard Blandford (his square tomb is in the churchyard), a local landowner owning around two thirds of the parish, who was a churchwarden at St Peter's, and also owned land around the King's Mead area of Gillingham. The three-light E. window, dedicated to Sidney, Lord Herbert of Lea, (1810–61) a benefactor of the church, was donated by his widow in 1861. Herbert, educated at Harrow and Oriel College, Oxford, became Conservative MP for South Wiltshire in 1832. Later, he was appointed to the Cabinet as secretary of war, under Lord Aberdeen's administration. During the Crimean campaign he saw many grave and appalling weaknesses in military administration and sought to improve them. A personal friend of Florence Nightingale, he was responsible for sending her out to ameliorate the sanitary conditions for the British Army at Scutari. This initiative developed into a movement which endeavoured to reform medical services and pressed for the greater education of army officers. Sidney Herbert was a much loved, admired and talented man. Following the stresses of the Crimean War he died, exhausted, at Wilton, where his monument can be seen in the chancel of the church of St Mary and St Nicholas.

All the stained and painted glass windows are Victorian. The beauty of the most outstanding window, dated 1882, is unfortunately lost to general view, sited as it is in the S. side vestry. None of the windows bear glassmakers marks or signatures.

The gem of a S. tower has double bell-openings; large and arched, divided by a Romanesque shaft. The stair-turret which rises above the battlements is topped with a conical spirelet. In the S. porch entrance is a mid-fourteenth-century carved armoured knight (preserved from the old church) which, still recumbent, now lies behind neo-Norman arches. The effigy possibly commemorates one Sir Thomas West; although a great deal appears to be known about him, there is little firm evidence for a positive identification of the figure. Immediately in front of the monument is a matrix in the stone floor, an indication of where there was once a brass to an Abbess. The Monumental Brass Society suggests, in an addendum to the church notes, that it was possibly from a Wilton or Shaftesbury monastery, placed here at the Dissolution for preservation and safety. A porch note records that it was one of only two brasses of Abbessess in England.

There being no bell-ringing chamber in the upper tower, the ropes from the three bells drop down into the S. porch entrance. The oldest bell of 1420–30, cast by Robert Crouch, was recast in 1881 and a facsimile of the original bell inscription now hangs on the S. wall – *Sancte Peetre ora pro nobis* – Saint Peter pray for us. The oldest of the present bells was cast in 1630.

It is the simplicity of the overall design and interior furnishings of this, so well tended and cared for, church which provoke such aesthetic pleasure; it is a joy and a delight.

TEMPLECOMBE
– East Somerset

On the A357, south of Wincanton.
O.S.Landranger 183.

Dedicated to Saint
Mary the Virgin

Combe Templariorum – Templecombe – the village taking its name from the Knights Templar connection, was the site of a major preceptory or commandery in the West of England (the Templar Order being given the land sometime before 1185, by Serlo FitzOdo, who was probably related to Odo, the Bishop of Bayeux, who originally held the land courtesy of William the Conquerer). Combe was included in the *Domesday Survey* of 1086 where part of it is shown as being held by the Bishop with his chaplain, Samson, holding it from him; the Saxon Earl Loefwin held the area before the Bishop.

The Parish of St Mary the Virgin comprises two distinct villages, now separated by the railway line from London to the West of England; Templecombe to the south and Abbas Combe to the north. The Manor Farm to the south of the village contains the few extant remains of the old commandery. The church notes, by Audrey Dymock Herdsman and A H Davies, provide a number of historical contexts. King Alfred the Great founded the Abbey dedicated to St Mary the Virgin in Shaftesbury in the year AD888, and one of his daughters, (to whom Asser, the Bishop of Sherborne and Alfred's biographer, gives the name Aethelgifu) became the first Abbess. *(See Shaftesbury.)* St Mary the Virgin in Combe became the daughter church to the nunnery in Shaftesbury, hence the name of the village – Abbas Combe and continued to receive the patronage of Shaftesbury until the Dissolution in 1539. (All other churches connected to the Mother House in Shaftesbury, were also dedicated to St Mary the Virgin).

The present church of St Mary the Virgin is most likely built on the site of the Saxon edifice. The embattled tower is positioned centrally but on the S. side of the nave. It is sturdy and handsome, with an attractive spirelet. Entrance to the nave is through the S. door set in the tower. The building is kept locked and anyone seeking entrance has to visit the Royal Wessex public house, during normal opening hours, to obtain the key. This public house where, reputedly, Queen Victoria once stayed overnight, is about two hundred yards south of the church, just beyond the railway bridge.

The nave has a very attractive fifteenth-century wagon roof and the W. door of the same period is still in situ. In 1834 the N. wall of the nave was removed and replaced with a four-bay arcade leading through to a very wide N. aisle of the same date.

The chancel is very spacious, having undergone rebuilding in 1865. It was then when the Norman E. window was replaced and the present five light arrangement inserted. Below it is a very finely carved reredos, whilst arching above them all is the splendid wagon roof. The area at the E. end of the nave, leading to the chancel, has fairly recently undergone a remodelling in a practical and contemporary style, allowing the communion rails to be easily removed providing an open area on a low, raised-dais for music recitals to take place.

There is some fine Victorian stained and painted glass but one of the outstanding memorials is the superb font cover with carving of great refinement. With an engraved copper dedicatory plate, (which is almost impossible to read because of where it is placed) it was donated in 1895 by Gertrude, a daughter of a previous rector, Thomas Fox. The square, elegant and impressive Norman-period font, on supports, is of Purbeck marble.

On the interior S. wall of the nave is a painted panel, now behind glass, which depicts a life-sized head of a bearded man, whose haunting face looks directly at the viewer in a most challenging and disturbing manner. The icon is sombre and mysterious, painted in muted tones in a style which one could reasonably state is medieval. Anyone gazing on the image, and being familiar with the Turin

Shroud may make the association, '... a man of sorrows and acquainted with grief,' as the Prophet Isaiah foretold.

The painting will be a startling discovery for anyone visiting St Mary's, but in 1945, it would undoubtedly have been that for Molly Drew who was the tenant of a cottage, off the High Street, Templecombe. Part of the plaster from the ceiling of an outhouse had fallen and, looking upwards, Mrs Drew saw the face looking down on her. A panel was discovered which had been secured by wires to the roof, and then the entire panel plastered over. One may reasonably assume it was an attempt to hide the panel but the important questions of 'when?' and 'why?' assert themselves. The then rector took possession of the panel from Mrs A Topp, the owner of the cottage, and after cleaning and restoration it was hung in the church in 1956. The information sheet available in the church states that the panel bears evidence of hinge marks and a keyhole, the conclusion being that it had been used as a door at some period; it goes on to record that the top of the panel is missing and draws attention to the fact that the icon has no halo around the head; a departure for religious genre painting. The presence of a halo, in the tradition of western religious art, indicates saintliness, but in the eastern tradition – power.

During the last few years the panel has been submitted for a carbon-14 dating process, the results of which revealed a date of c.1280. The similarity between the Turin Shroud and the Templecombe panel has led to a theory that it was the Templars who brought back the Shroud from Jerusalem, during the crusades, and made copies from it such as the one here.

Into this intriguing story an 'however' insinuates itself; a large 'however', and the possibility of the panel having connections with the icon on the Turin Shroud becomes very doubtful. Helen Nicholson tackles this problem in her investigative volume into the Templars, from the Order's beginnings in around 1120 through to its dissolution in 1312. *The Knights Templar*, specifically mentions the Templecombe painting and the misconception of it being an icon of Christ. Dr Nicholson explains that two German Masters of the Templar Order had Christ's head on their seals (Christ was the king of the Order, after all), but elsewhere the Templars used, '… the image of the *agnus dei*, the lamb of God, to represent Christ, and in all the rest of the surviving Templar iconography there are no bearded heads of Christ or anyone else …'. However, she goes on to state that, 'The Hospitallers of St John did venerate a bearded head, that of St John the Baptist which appears on the seals of the order in England. It also appears elsewhere in Hospitaller iconography in Britain, for example in the medieval painting of a bearded head now in the church at Templecombe in Somerset.' So perhaps the image is that of John the Baptist?

The most up-to-date scientific evidence, published in the late 1980s, shows the date of the Turin Shroud, most likely a painted image, to have been made within a time scale of the 1320s to 1330s; forty to fifty years after the dating of the Templecombe panel to 1280. It is therefore possible to imagine that the image relates to an icon of John the Baptist relevant to the Knights Hospitaller Order, who, when they took over the commandery or preceptory at Templecombe, may have brought it with them, sometime after 1312.

Was it when the Knights Hospitallers lost possession of Templecombe at the Dissolution of the Monasteries in 1539–40, that the painted panel was hidden in the ceiling of the outhouse? After the Dissolution the preceptory passed to the crown and, eventually, into private ownership.

This still raises a number of questions. Even if one accepts that it has associations with the Knights Hospitaller, rather than the Knights Templar, there is still the question of the panel's provenance and, further, is it a copy of a master image? In spite of its medieval artistic appearance, the image appears to possess aspects of eastern iconography. It is known that western trained artists combined western art medium with eastern styles which rather supports that observation. Its underlying austere asceticism shows a denial of the body in favour of spiritual enlightenment gained through an eremitical way of life. The original master image, if that was the case, may have been an eastern icon from a much earlier period.

One piece of internal evidence from the panel perhaps reveals a tentative connection with the rich and powerful maritime state of

Venice. The head is depicted within a painted frame of unusual design which probably represents the charger or platter upon which the head of John the Baptist was presented to Salomé. The form of this charger is fundamentally a square with the four corners aligned to the cardinal points of a compass rose and on each face of the square a hemisphere extruding externally. This interesting form manifests itself in Venetian art and may, conjecturally, reveal a Byzantine influence on its style. In the Basilica of San Marco one of the world's greatest art treasures, the *Pala d'Oro*, a gold, enamel and jewel-encrusted panel, acts as a background or reredos to the altar. In the direct centre of the upper tier of this large, complex work is an enamel and gold icon of the Archangel Michael surrounded by a frame in a form directly akin to the one in Templecombe.

The *Pala d'Oro* is a masterpiece of the Venetian Gothic goldsmith's art. It is strongly believed that the upper tier of the panel was constructed from the spoils following the merciless sack of Constantinople, the culmination of the diverted Fourth crusade (1201–4) which was described, in *The Fourth Crusade* by Jonathan Phillips, by one eye-witness, Niketas Choniates, as '... madmen raging against the sacred.' The crusaders were Western Christians who attacked brother and sister Eastern Christians perpetrating every atrocity imaginable – sacking churches, smashing altars and plundering precious and sacred objects. (In 2001, Pope John Paul II apologised to the Greek Orthodox Church for the abomination.) Venice, the *Porta Orientalis*, gateway to the east, was an important trading link at a halfway point between the Holy Land and the Northern European countries of England, Germany and France.

In *The Oxford History of the Crusades*, 'Art in the Latin East 1098–1291', Jaroslav Folda explains, 'The appearance of icon painting as an important new medium of crusader art is most apparent between 1250 and 1291.' Folda goes on to state, referring to an icon of the crucifixion, that it was, 'Probably done by *an artist of Venetian background*, [my italics] the iconography is a combination of Byzantine and Frankish elements ...', and continues, in connection with a painting of the Virgin and Child, that it '... was done by a crusader painter in the manner of Italian thirteenth-century painting under the influence of Byzantine icons.'

It was in the important Christian city and commercial port of Acre, between 1250–91, that crusader art flourished, before the city was besieged and fell.

There are numerous possibilities regarding the provenance of the panel therefore no firm conclusions can or should be made on the above fragmented observations. A bona-fide art historian with expertise in this genre and period could probably provide a more definitive answer.

Pilgrims to the holy places were frequently attacked by the followers of Islam and a small number of knights devoted themselves to protect them, forming a religious community for that express purpose around 1120. The Knights Templar, or, Order of the Poor Knights of Christ and of the Temple of Solomon, was one of three orders of knighthood created at the time of the crusades; the others being the Order of the Hospital of St John of Jerusalem and the Knights of the Teutonic Order (The Order of St Mary of the Germans). These were specifically religious orders and the most important founded in the Holy Land at that time. However, other orders of knighthood were also founded but they did not have a religious foundation.

In the beginning the Templars swore obedience to the Patriarch of Jerusalem, taking vows of poverty, chastity and obedience (adopting the rules of the Benedictine Order). The then King of Jerusalem, Baldwin II (ruled 1118–31), gave the knights accommodation in part of the royal palace around the area of the Jewish Temple, near to where the Aqsa mosque stands on the Temple Mount – hence their name. The Templars drew up their own rule and customs, approved at a church council. Within the order were three groups: knights, sergeants and priests. The sergeants were comprised of military men who were not knights, 'men-at-arms' would be a more appropriate term, craftsmen and servants. The priests were also called chaplains. There were sisters, but they were not represented in Britain. Only the knights, who were of noble birth, wore the white mantle with a red cross on the shoulder. The larger number of sergeants wore black.

(The Hospitallers also wore black and had two crosses; a white version with eight points, the famous Maltese Cross, and a red cross with four arms but no splayed or flattened ends. The first version was worn on the habit, the second used on the field of battle. The Teutonic Order also wore black with a white mantle bearing a black cross so it is hardly surprising that much confusion arose regarding the differences of the orders. Even contemporaries appear to have referred to them all as Templars.) The Templar Order was ruled by a Grand Master who could not make major decisions without the assent of a general chapter comprised of thirteen members. Every commandery, or temple, of the order was overseen by a Commander who, in turn, owed his obedience to the Grand Master. If the Templars possessed more than one establishment in a particular country (the order became Europe wide) the local commanders were then subordinate to a Grand Commander, sometimes referred to as Visitor or Preceptor.

In addition to learning and practising the arts of war, the Templars also had spiritual duties to attend, being monks as well as soldiers. The taking of Mass, said by one of the Templar priests was an obligatory part of the daily routine. The cottage where the Templecombe icon was discovered was originally part of a priest's house relating to the preceptory or commandery.

The loss of Acre in 1291 was a major setback for the Templars. Dr Nicholson points out that it was a great psychological blow, because with it went the Order's base in the Holy Land; it also lost its fighting men, equipment and fortresses into which vast resources had been poured.

Rumours had begun to circulate regarding the Templars, maliciously designed for no other purpose than to bring the Order into disrepute. The pious Philip IV, King of France was outwardly on good terms with the Templars. However, Philip had most likely become alarmed at Templar power, the Order having become extremely wealthy because of their ability to handle their business affairs with great competence (in fact they were responsible for the rise in banking in Western Europe). He may have coveted their power and wealth, particularly as he was desperately short of money; but much of Templar wealth lay in property and equipment.

'It thus came as a complete shock,' suggests Helen Nicholson, 'to almost everyone when on the 13th of October 1307 the Templar Brothers in France were arrested on the order of King Philip IV ... the Brothers were imprisoned and interrogated on a number of charges.'

Pope Clement V was outraged at Philip IV's arrest of the Templars because it had occurred without his consent. (Only the Pope could assent to the arrest of a religious order.) Clement declared that he was aware of the circulating rumours and said, in his own defence, that an investigation was planned. Thus, pushed into action, in November 1307 he sent out letters to all the kings of Western Christendom who were in no position to ignore their contents; they could not oppose either the Pope or Philip IV.

The innocence of the Templars in the face of the many charges brought against them at their trial is, by the consent of modern historians, well proven. Helen Nicholson shows that the charges were carefully constructed, stemming from popular myth relating to heresy and magic. Heresy was a large and convenient peg on which to hang numerous phobias – anything which does not conform to the accepted beliefs of society, any deviation and eccentricity departing from the norm, a catch-all in which many thousands of people could easily become entrapped. (Many modern parallels can be seen here.) Christians believed that if heretics were not destroyed, the destruction of society would logically follow. God would punish all Christians if they did not punish heresy and such fears gathered pace from the eleventh century.

The charges against the Templars fell into two categories: errors of belief and errors of practice. In the first category it was stated that the Templars denied Christ when they were received into the Order, or shortly afterwards. They offered adoration of a cat (because cats were seen wandering around Templar buildings!), they spat on the cross and defiled it, members exchanged kisses of an obscene nature upon being received into the Order, they practised sodomy and they did not believe in the Mass or other sacraments. Into the second category it was declared that the Order made no donations of charitable gifts nor did they offer hospitality and they did not consider it a sin to acquire property belonging to others by legal or illegal means. The catalogue of charges in both categories ran on and on. This body of 'evidence' was brought by the French authorities when the brothers came to trial.

The English King, Edward II (1307–1327) ordered the arrest of the Templars from the forty to fifty commanderies in England, including the brothers at Templecombe, even though he did not believe the charges. However, he was in no position to disagree considering that he desired papal support to continue pursuing his war in Scotland.

Helen Nicholson states that the pope sent investigators of heresy from France to England to press King Edward into consenting to torture being used upon the English brothers in order to gain confessions. In December 1309 he finally agreed to the pope's request but no one was prepared to use torture. In fact the Templar brothers were generally well treated. Three brothers in London confessed but confessions are sometimes made in the simple belief that that would be the end of the matter. In the Diocese of York no torture was used and no brothers confessed; they were allowed to swear their innocence. This was in complete contrast to France where torture was routinely used.

I am particularly grateful to Dr Helen Nicholson who is currently producing a major study, *The Trial of the Templars in the British Isles*; she has provided me with the following information. The arrested brothers were sent from Templecombe to the Tower of London. William de Burton, the last commander here, had been in charge of the preceptory for four years. Prior to that he had been at Temple Balsall in Warwickshire, situated between and south of Solihull and Coventry where he had been received into the order in 1305. Three of the other brothers from Templecombe who were arrested with the commander were John de Ivel, Walter de Rokele and Roger de Wyke (who was probably a member of the Wyke family of Wyke near Gillingham, during the reign of Edward III [see Hutchins]). Roger never reached the Tower because he died on 15 April 1308; the cause of his death unknown.

William de Burton was interrogated in late 1309 and again in February 1310. He stated that the order was free of heresy but he did admit that he knew nothing of the Templars' practices outside England which indicates that he had not been outside of England and certainly not to the East. In March 1310 he was examined again with others of the order from the province of Canterbury, and again in June 1310. On Monday 12 July 1311 he appeared with many other Templars before the Archbishop of Canterbury, other bishops and the Earls of Leicester, Hereford and Pembroke and a large crowd where he made a formal statement renouncing all heresies. He was given a light sentence of doing penance. It is suggested that this was probably because he had been in the order for only four years. He was sent to John, Bishop of Lincoln to be assigned to live in a religious house, to undertake his penance.

John de Aley (or Ivel), most likely Brother John of Euley (or Ule) said, in November 1309, that he had been received into the order at Temple Balsall in July 1306. However, William de Burton, when being examined in March 1310, stated that John de Ule had died after the first examination but he did not say how or why that had happened.

Walter de Rokele (or Rokely) had been received into the order earlier in 1302 again at Temple Balsall. Walter was examined for a second time in February 1310 when he stated that the order was not heretical but added that he knew nothing about the rule of the order due to the fact that he, as a layman, could not read; possibly meaning that he could not read Latin, as many lay people could read their own language by this time. He was interrogated again in March 1310 when he stated that he had never been presented at a reception ceremony except his own. In June 1310 he was interrogated once more, together with other Templars from the province of York and stated that he had never been at a general chapter meeting of the order; not perhaps surprising for a low-ranking brother. He appeared again on Friday 9th July, 1311 in the lodging of the Dean of St Paul's, London, with twelve others, in the presence of the Bishops of London and Chichester. The group explained that they had not been in the order very long and had never been present at a general chapter meeting (therefore they could not have been involved at the alleged heretical practices). Later that day the same group with five other Templars appeared before the Archbishop of Canterbury, Bishops, other religious, clergy and the people of London, in the Bishop's Hall, Southwark, where they solemnly renounced all heresies. On this occasion they were formally absolved and given penances to perform. Walter de Rokely was sent to the Bishop of Winchester to be assigned to a religious house to undertake his penance.

William de Burton and Walter de Rokely lived until at least 1338. We know this because their names were listed among former Templars whose pensions were still being paid by the Knights Hospitaller in England. The Hospitallers had to pay for the support of former Templars even though a great majority of them were living in the houses of other religious orders (not in the houses of Hospitallers).

Templar commanderies and their lands were taken into the King's hands when the Templars were arrested from 19 January, 1308. The commanderies were entrusted to a royal keeper, made responsible for collecting its revenues and paying its debts. When the King wanted money or goods for specific purposes, for example his pursuit of the war against Scotland, he would contact his royal keeper. In the 1307 to 1313 *Calendar of the Close Rolls* of Edward II there is an instruction, dated 28 July 1312, issued by the treasurers and barons of the exchequer (royal treasury officials). (*Close Rolls* were mandates, letters and writs of a private nature, addressed in the sovereign's name to individuals, and folded or 'closed' and sealed on the outside with the Great Seal of the Realm.) The instruction was addressed to the keeper of the Templars' lands in County Somerset ordering him to award Alexander de Hunsingore (not of the Templar brotherhood) the following, '… that he ought to receive for life: his food at the brothers' table in the Templars' house in Cumbe, a suitable robe for a clerk or esquire at Christmas yearly, a mark sterling yearly [a mark is two thirds of a pound] with the service of a groom, and hay and oats for his horse … for so long as the said Alexander labours about the affairs of the house, and when he can no longer labour, the said prebend [a tithe, providing it] of the oats shall be withdrawn and thereafter he is to be satisfied with hay for his horse if he have one, and he is to give one half of his goods to the house at his death.'

The 1313 to 1318 *Close Rolls* of Edward II record that on 9 December 1313 the King announced that he had handed over to the representative of the Hospital of St John of Jerusalem, Brother Leonard de Tibertis, Prior of Venice and Proctor-General of the Hospitallers, all the former property of the Templars in his realms. Leonard de Tibertis was visiting England at this time and it is known that he travelled throughout England during his visit and would have spent some time at Clerkenwell, the Hospitallers headquarters. (However, King Edward's declaration was not strictly correct as he had in fact already given much Templar property to his friends and nobles, and property which had been taken back by the families who had given it to the Templars was not returned to the Hospitallers).

The 1330 to 1333 *Close Rolls* of Edward III (reigned from 1327) show that on 15 December 1332 the King instructed that the sheriff of Somerset hand over to the Hospital, among other properties in Somerset, the manor of Templecombe, which was occupied by Geoffrey de Stawell. The Stawell family were important landowners in the county.

A report of 1338 from Philip de Thame, Grand Prior of England, sent to the Grand Master and Convent of the Hospital on Rhodes, Hélion de Villeneuve, outlines the financial situation of the Hospital in England. From this report the names of three Hospitaller brothers at Templecombe can be extracted: Brother Robert de Nafford, knight and the commander at Templecombe at that time, Robert de Estrete (possibly an English name given a French spelling) and John de Wherwell.

At this time there were only three Hospitaller Brothers, specifically named above, but earlier in the Hospitaller period the number of Brothers had been higher. The report also lists a number of job descriptions for non-Hospitaller personnel at Templecombe: chaplain, carpenter, cook, key-holder, janitor, clerk, reaper and two 'lads'. Helen Nicholson points out that staffing arrangements during the Knights Templar tenure would have been very similar. (The report also records that the Hospitallers' house at Chippenham in Wiltshire, was the largest in England, with ten brothers).

We can firmly reject notions of knights galloping around on horseback, practising the arts of warfare. It is here that fact has to get in the way of a good romantic derring-do story. To maintain the presence of both orders, in the Holy Land and elsewhere, required very large amounts of money; it was the function of the commandery here to recruit new members and raise funds from the proceeds of farming and other allied business activities. No swords, no armour, no lances; nothing but a continual seasonal cycle of breeding and raising animals, and whatever else was necessary as part of their farming activities. Their land holding was extensive (Bristol being part of their responsibility), with much of it rented out for farming.

※※※

I am indebted to Dr Greg O'Malley, whose study, *The Knights Hospitaller of the English Langue 1460 to 1565*, is to be published shortly. Dr O'Malley has provided the names of a number of commanders who served at Templecombe, some of whom had spent ten to fifteen years in Rhodes before being appointed to a preceptory. There would have been many opportunities for them to obtain Greek religious art. Generally speaking, some of them developed ties of service and friendship with Greeks, even bringing them back to Britain, some to act as administrators and some as servants.

William Dawney, a Yorkshireman, was appointed to Templecombe during the 1450s but returned to Rhodes in 1458. At that time he was an important figure in the Hospitaller order who held a number of military commands and diplomatic posts. He served as Captain of Bodrum in 1448–9 and was Visitor to Cos in 1452.

Marmaduke Lumley probably belonged to a well known Co.Durham family. He was in Rhodes in the late 1450s and early 60s and was present at the relief of Rhodes in 1481 following its siege by the Turks in 1480. Lumley was at Templecombe in the mid 1460s.

Walter Fitzherbert, probably of Norbury, Derbyshire. He was in

Rhodes in 1470, 74, 78–9 and 88–89, where he died in 1489. Fitzherbert was appointed to Templecombe in November 1478 and was granted a licence to return home to run his preceptory on 19 February 1479.

Robert Dalison was in Rhodes in December 1478 and appointed to Templecombe on 20 June 1489. He exchanged Templecombe for the preceptory at Shingay, Cambridgeshire in May 1502. Dalison was in Rhodes in March 1489 and 1501–3.

Lancelot Docwra of Kirkby Kendall, Westmoreland. He was appointed to Templecombe on 6 February 1503. Docwra died in 1520.

Nicholas Fairfax, a Yorkshireman, was in Rhodes in 1506, a year after being received into the order and remained there until 1521. Although he was appointed to Templecombe in June 1521, it is unlikely that he ever took up his post. Fairfax died in Rome impoverished and 'stark mad' in April 1523.

Richard Neville was in Rhodes in 1522 and appointed commander at Templecombe in addition to Willoughton, Lincolnshire on 8 May 1523. He remained in his posts for only a brief period and died in March 1528.

Edmund Hussey of Shapwick, Dorset, was received into the order, in Viterbo, Italy in 1524. His father was Thomas Hussee *(sic)* whose brother Nicholas, a knight of Rhodes i.e. a member of the Hospitaller Order, was appointed commander of Ansty, Wiltshire in 1524. Edmund's *(shown as Edward in Hutchins)* younger brother James is also recorded as a knight of Rhodes. (A full pedigree of Husey, or Hussey, of Shapwick and of Thompson, Co. Dorset is shown in Hutchins.) Edmund was appointed to Templecombe on 6 March 1528. He is a very important figure, being the last commander of Templecombe before the 1540 Dissolution. If the panel was hidden immediately prior to the Dissolution then it is possible that as commander he may have known of, or been party to the deed. Was it hidden for the purpose of concealing it from the king's commissioners; for saving it for a future generation to discover; or for personal reasons?

Some Hospitallers hoped that their preceptories would re-open at a future date. In fact, the year 1540 was *not* the end of the Hospitaller preceptory at Templecombe. Mary I (reigned 1553–1558), singlemindedly set out to restore the old order, including the Latin Mass and the acceptance of papal supremacy. In 1557, during the brief resurgence of Roman Catholicism, Cardinal Reginald Pole was authorised, by royal letters patent, to restore the order. Templecombe was one of nine preceptories in crown possession, which reopened and flourished for a little over one year. The last actual commander was **James Shelley** of Michelgrove in Sussex. He was admitted to the order in 1557 and granted the preceptory at Templecombe; probably chosen because he was already known to Mary, Philip or Cardinal Pole for the capabilities he had demonstrated in some capacity in their service. The protestant Elizabeth I (reigned 1558–1603) was crowned queen in January 1559 and the preceptory was closed in March 1559 – forever. Following the final closure of Templecombe, Shelley appears in Malta until September 1561 and again in 1577.

The list of Hospitaller commanders reveals how some had travelled widely before being appointed to Templecombe; the gazetteer of places is impressive. Some of the men who had been active in those places had held positions of great responsibility, Dawney, for example, held diplomatic status and had numerous dealings with the Turks. The fact that men such as Dawney were appointed to Templecombe suggests that this preceptory was of significance and the fact that it was one of a small number to be re-opened, supports that observation.

It is because of the painting displayed in the church that these interesting characters connected with the preceptory become more tangible to us. Couple that with the possibility that any one of them may have had a link with it, bringing it here as part of their baggage. It is a very stirring story full of possibilities.

❊❊❊

Whatever personal recollections one carries away from St Mary's, Templecombe, the challenging face on the painted panel, whoever it may represent, is one which can almost certainly be guaranteed to remain imprinted on the memory.

TISBURY
– South-West Wiltshire

South-east of Hindon (B3089).
O.S.Landranger 184.

Dedicated to Saint John the Baptist

Are you aware that Tisbury and Chilmark are close to Martha's Vineyard?

Majestically encircled is St John's, Tisbury, not by standing Megaliths, but by the deep-rooted, aristocratic Taxus baccata, the Yew tree. One of them, of great longevity is possibly four thousand years old, many of the others merely centuries. The Yew, a symbol of pre-Christian religion and burial places, once used to fashion the deadly English Longbow, here peacefully provides shade, dappling the verdant sward with sliding shadows thrown by the searching noonday sun. The passing centuries have not substantially altered the scene, its propinquity still waiting quietly for those who visit with eyes, imagination and perception to see it with the inner eye. Here, in the lovely churchyard, near to the south-east corner of the church, are the graves of John Lockwood and Alice Kipling, parents of the writer Rudyard Kipling who lived in the village. Local lore runs that Kipling wrote *The Jungle Book* here.

St John's is marginally off the village centre, its central tower easily and clearly visible from the train to or from London. *A History of the Parish Church of St John the Baptist, Tisbury* by Rex Sawyer, (available in the church) tells the visitor that it is of the twelfth century, but little remains of that period. However, it is highly probable that much earlier buildings occupied this long venerated and sacred site.

A first impression on gaining the interior is to experience an exciting architectural venture, a combination of concepts; ancient and modern. The building becomes interesting by the creation of a spatial division into two large separate areas of worship. St John's is a large cruciform shaped building, its lofty nave in the Perp. style, having clerestory windows above which is a fine wagon roof, restored in the twentieth century, with lovely hammer beams bearing carved angels carrying shields. There is a general overall feeling of spaciousness, the church's size reflecting large congregations and ambitions of earlier periods. The nave accommodates the altar beneath the tower crossing, therefore it is not separated, in the conventional sense, from the chancel by clergy and choir stalls, the latter now installed in the E. end of the S. transept; it brings the altar, and by obvious association the ritual, closer to the congregation. If religious ritual is drama (not entertainment), which it is or should be with its mysteries and language, then here is the perfect setting for drama and mystery to unfold and be revealed.

To proceed from the nave into what was the Dec. Period chancel, eastwards beyond and behind the tower crossing, is to experience a spiritual and aesthetic change of gear. The area is now designated a chapel, specifically dedicated to St Andrew in 1974; and how noble and dignified it is. The concept of ancient nave and modernised E. end chapel within this village church is a touch of genius. All those individuals involved in making and taking such a bold decision are to be congratulated for their foresight and conviction. To enter through the glass doors is profoundly affecting. The chapel is filled, on bright days, with a light of a powerful intensity, increasing thereby the contrast with the sombre nave. To quote from the guide, 'The chancel is rich in historical interest.'; certainly no over statement.

For the visitor with a penchant for memorials the chancel and sanctuary will provide a feast. Here are memorials to local and national figures, side by side in perpetuity. There is an outstanding brass to Edmund Hyde and one to Lawrence Hyde, his wife, six sons and four daughters. Many of the tablets relate to the Arundell family, who apart from the 5th and 8th barons are interred in the now closed vault below. There are so many Arundells to choose from; their acts well recorded. For example, take Sir Thomas Arundell, owner of the Manor and

Castle of Wardour, executed for felony in 1552. His grandson, also Thomas, became the first Lord Arundell. It was the latter's daughter, Ann, who married Lord Baltimore, the founder of the American State of Maryland. He was granted the territory in 1632 by King Charles I and it was Charles' wife, Queen Henrietta Maria whose name is perpetuated in the name of the State. Baltimore is the State's largest city and port on Chesapeake Bay; Annapolis is the state capital and Arundell County, an administrative division.

According to Rex Sawyer, there exists a verbal tradition relating to the stained-glass in the E. window which runs, that it was designed by Sir Christopher Wren. His father, Dr Christopher Wren, Rector of East Knoyle and also a trained architect, was commissioned by Queen Henrietta Maria to design a building for her. *(See East Knoyle.)* In view of Ann Arundell's family connections with St John's, Tisbury, and Henrietta Maria's connections with Dr Wren, does the foregoing add weight to the tradition that Christopher Wren designed the window?

The element which links the east and west, is the tower crossing. The tower itself is internally supported on four architecturally transitional Norman piers *c.*1180–1200. The capitals are decorated with scallop designs, thought by Pevsner to be coarse, but possibly intended to be carved later. Above is the bell-stage with a ring of six bells. Number 3 bell (1720) bears the inscription, *GOD PRESERVE THE CHURCH. Wm COCKEY CAST MEE*; number 4 bell (1783) is inscribed, *Wm BILBIE CHEWSTOKE FECIT*. William Bilbie of Chewstoke, Somerset cast bells from 1698 to 1814. Externally the top stage, embattled with four obelisk corner pinnacles bearing a vane atop each, carries the three dial clock installed in 1925 when a major rebuilding took place. If the top stage is slightly eccentric, it is that eccentricity which makes it interesting. The tower originally supported a sixty-foot spire which in 1762, due to a lightning strike, crashed down through the N. transept and aisle; the second time in twenty years. It was following the second disaster that the top stage was then added.

The S. aisle has two outstanding stained-glass windows, one, *The Baptism of Our Lord*, marking the fiftieth year of the incumbency of Revd F E Hutchinson and the other commemorating a former church organist of forty-four years, Edwin Osmond and his wife Maria. This window bears a wonderfully evocative image of six choristers in purple cassocks and white surplices; their well scrubbed, earnest and handsome features finely drawn. The whole window, filled with subtle colour, is a very fine period piece. The S. aisle is a place to linger and reflect for some time on the many brasses and memorial tablets, including one to those parishioners who fell in WWI.

The guide draws attention to the Lady Chapel at the E. end of the N. transept. It was first dedicated in 1299 and celebrated its 700th anniversary in 1999. This fact gives pause for reflection again, if only momentarily, upon the long time span of continuous worship here and the local, national and world events during those long, and some long distant, centuries. A very fine window donated by Clara Giles, in memory of her Bracher grandparents, is complemented on either side by well carved niches of the fifteenth and sixteenth century which bear New Testament and other saintly figures. The arched recess built into the window behind the altar carries a statue of the Blessed Virgin and Child to whom the chapel is dedicated.

St John's begs the visitor to return, as there is so much to entrance and delight the eye, for the intellect to contemplate and understand and for the spirit to be uplifted by. Craftsmanship abounds in the Jacobean pulpit and pews, the carved bosses and floor brasses in the N. aisle, the lists of priests and incumbents from 1299, the W. and E. windows and the finely embroidered, multi-coloured, multi-patterned hassocks or kneelers, hand wrought between 1972 and 1986 – the undertaking being inspired by Audrey Chorley; a tribute of devotion and love both by herself and her team of needlewomen.

The Mayhew family are well established in the Tisbury area and have been since the thirteenth century. Around 1630 one Thomas Mayhew emigrated to the New World, settling in Massachusetts in 1632; by 1641 he was able to purchase Martha's Vineyard Island. North Tisbury, West Tisbury and Chilmark are still used as place names thus perpetuating the connection with the Old Country.

TOLLARD ROYAL
– South-West Wiltshire

On the B3081, south-west of Shaftesbury.
O.S.Landranger 184.

Dedicated to Saint
Peter ad Vincula

Tollard Royal, the heart
and head of Cranborne
Chase, one of the most outstandingly beautiful landscapes of
England, is Pitt-Rivers country and Cranborne Chase is where
scientific discipline and rational methods in archaeology in Britain
began. Pitt-Rivers or more specifically, General Augustus Henry
Lane Fox Pitt-Rivers, is a name long respected and honoured by all
foremost British and foreign university departments of archaeology;
he pioneered the way, laying the foundations for what are now
fundamental standard practices in field-archaeology and the church
St Peter ad Vincula is where he is particularly remembered.

St Peter ad Vincula (St Peter in chains) stands in close proximity to
King John's House, which formerly belonged to General Pitt-Rivers,
described by Nicholas Pevsner as 'memorable'; indeed it is. However,
the General, having excavated around the house discovered no
evidence to link it with King John. The House was open to the public,
when owned by Pitt-Rivers but is now in private ownership. It has,
therefore, to be admired from a discreet distance. The church has been
much renewed, e.g. almost the entire chancel was rebuilt and the N.
aisle added before the 1870s. The embattled W. tower is sturdy and
low, having crocketed corner pinnacles, simple louvred bell-openings
and a clear glazed W. window. The S. porch entrance, constructed of
alternating courses of flint and masonry, is particularly attractive, one
can feel its weight, heavy with years.

It would be understandable to seek out only General Pitt-Rivers'
memorial, but that would be to miss some other very poignant wall
memorial tablets. In the N. aisle, E. end is a marble memorial

dedicated to the memory of George Pitt-Rivers and his wife Susan Georgiana; he died on 28 April, she on 30 April 1866. The perfectly apt text, chosen to illustrate their life-long love and the fact they died within two days of each other, is taken from II Samuel 1:23:

They were lovely and pleasant in their lives,
and in their death they were not divided.

The superb E. window, also dedicated to their memory, suffuses the chancel with an intense and rich light. The essence of the inscription reads, 'George Pitt-Rivers, Baron Rivers of Sudeley Castle, Born 1810, his wife Susan Georgiana Leveson-Gower *(Dukes of Sutherland)* born the same year.' Whilst in the N. aisle do note the E. window dedicated to Alice Arbuthnot, which is quite splendid; not English but by Bert(oll)ini of Milan (1867). Giuseppe Bert(oll)ini, along with a number of other continental stained-glass painters, exhibited his work at the Great Exhibition of 1851, as a result of which he received a number of commissions. This window is a well known and recorded work. Alice Arbuthnot was struck and killed by lightning on 26 June 1865 whilst on the Schildhorn Alp, Switzerland. This accident took place only eight weeks after her marriage here at St Peter ad Vincula. Placed on the E. wall is a cruciform shaped brass case, holding a simple wooden cross made by local Swiss people to mark the spot where the fatality occurred. The cross was recovered, brought home and placed here in her memory.

In the central bay of the arcade, between the nave and N. aisle is a carved stone, cross-legged and recumbent effigy of a knight, Sir William Payne (d.1388). The figure is holding his damaged stone shield; the field decorated with three lozenges. It shows signs of iconoclastic acts of vandalism in churches; so often Parliamentarian in origin, which were perpetrated during the Civil War.

Rediscovered and uncovered in 1961 are a number of wall paintings on the S. wall of the nave which show texts, cartouches and a splendidly painted, animated angel playing a trumpet. Pevsner records their date as seventeenth-century but they may be somewhat earlier i.e., *c*.late-sixteenth-century. They were probably painted over, at the latest, in the early seventeenth-century, as demanded by law.

At the W. end of the nave is a memorial to General Pitt-Rivers and his wife. This takes the form of a well proportioned and decorated semicircular arch of carved marble, set within which is a black marble casket. Centrally mounted on the casket is a circular medallion depicting the General's life, in iconic form: a theodolite, pick, skull, urn, and what is probably an axe head. He favoured cremation, which was quite unusual at that time, the idea horrifying most people.

Augustus Henry Lane-Fox (1827–1900) was born in Yorkshire, but on inheriting his Great-Uncle's estate of Rushmore, Cranborne Chase (1880), he added, as a condition of his inheritance, Pitt-Rivers to his name. He was educated at Sandhurst and commissioned into the Grenadier Guards, rising to the rank of lieutenant-general. Pitt-Rivers was responsible for introducing the rifle into the British army and became involved in the testing and modification of various models. From that sprang an interest in the development of weapons and then the development of tools. The General is credited with the first real steps towards a scientific method in archaeology, which was revolutionary at that time. Following the inheritance of his part of Cranborne Chase, and retired from the army, he set about excavating the, as he suspected, potentially rich and widespread ancient monuments on his estate. Some of his excavations, in Wiltshire and in Dorset, were on a very large scale, needing both careful control and meticulous recording of data. He excavated each site in full, recording the exact position of each and every artefact; nothing was too minute for consideration. It was the completely ordinary, everyday remains which fascinated him (he was certainly no treasure hunter), for to him those small remains were the keys to past human activity. Importantly, it was Pitt-Rivers who developed the layer by layer stratigraphic technique, and further, he published his findings promptly and in detail, which is more than can be said of some more modern or contemporary archaeologists. His *Excavations in Cranborne Chase, 1887–98*, is a classic in archaeology. It took some time for his techniques to be generally adopted by others, some of whom still continued to excavate using the 'digging for potatoes' method. He was elected Fellow of the Royal Society in 1876, one of his sponsors being Charles Darwin. General Pit-Rivers died at Rushmore in 1900. Because of his careful methods, attention to detail and rational mind, his contributions to anthropology and archaeology were enormous, not only is he the Father of British Archaeology he is also of outstanding international importance in the same disciplines.

Sir Mortimer Wheeler wrote of him, 'From the miserable scraps of ancient humanity which his spade was constantly bringing to light, information had to be wrung drop by drop by sheer intellectual grasp, by an imagination that found its exercise in an enlarged understanding of the manifestations and processes of ordinary, unheroic human destiny.'

UPTON NOBLE
– East Somerset

On the A359, north of Bruton.
O.S.Landranger 183.

Dedicated to Saint Mary Magdalene

A tiny building in every aspect, overlooking a superb, entirely rural panorama, with not a trace of industrialisation in sight; result, simple human pleasure.

St Mary Magdalene is located at a slightly higher elevation than the visitor as he or she approaches through the lychgate. The church is charming in all its French-style rustic simplicity, the building would sit ill-at-ease in any other setting; an architecture born out of a pastoral environment.

The small guide book published by the enterprising Frome Society for Local Study and written for them by Michael McGarvie FSA, offers a well researched and comprehensive literary tour of the church, its background and surrounding environment. Upton Noble has a symbolic ring to it; Old English – *Upptun* – a high settlement. As one might reasonably expect the habitation is recorded in the *Domesday Survey* of 1086, being owned then by the Bishop of Coutance, and referred to as *Opetone*. Geoffrey of Montbray, Bishop of Coutance (1049–1093), fought at Hastings and was an active member of the King's government. Because of his preferment he became the seventh-richest of King William's supporters outside the Royal Family. The Bishop became involved in a rebellion of 1088 but in his case he was pardoned, after initially losing his possessions which were eventually restored to him.

In AD940 Batcombe was given to Glastonbury Abbey and it is likely, suggests the guide, that although the monks never acquired Upton it was they who erected the church in the twelfth century, serving it from Batcombe. There is a flavour of a French, country building to its style. Of that Norman Period building only the S. doorway and some fittings still remain. The unconventional tower with its saddleback roof was added in the thirteenth century, the doorway style used as evidence for that date. The church was enlarged around 1500 with the addition of a S. aisle, followed about one hundred years later by the addition of larger windows.

Following the English Civil War (1642–1651) Batcombe and Upton passed to the Puritans who stamped their authority and ritual practices upon the parish. However, in 1662, following the Act of Uniformity, the Book of Common Prayer became common usage and the Puritan clergyman was ejected from his living because he would not comply. Nevertheless Puritan tradition remained and Holy Communion at St Mary's continued to be taken seated around a table. The Puritans also had a general predilection for the same Sacrament being administered from pew to pew. It was with the arrival of the Revd Thomas Coney (1790–1840) that these practices ceased.

Sadly, in keeping with other churches in rural areas, St Mary Magdalene became seriously neglected. Around 1785, a description prepared for *Collinson's History* stated, 'The church is a small edifice much out of repair, 38 feet in length & 24 in width, consisting of a nave, chancel & south aile [sic] with a quadangular old tower over the porch which also serves as a belfry and contains two bells. The pews & seats are old & ordinary, the floor bad, the walls green & damp & the whole very dirty.' 'A grim word picture …' observes Michael McGarvie. The following century the fabric can be seen in a very parlous condition, the evidence this time provided by a faded photograph. For example it was recorded in a letter to the *Western Gazette* in 1876 that a pew collapsed whilst three people were sitting on it! From the following year, 1877, comes another very telling letter, to the same newspaper, which draws attention to the richness of the living at Upton Noble amounting to £1200 per annum, ' … is it a fact that they can't raise £200 out of this enormous sum to repair the church …?' The letter proceeds to question the justice of selfish land owning interests, pretended care for the cause of religion, anomalies of rich livings, starving curates and ruined churches.

Material salvation manifested itself through Revd William Collyns Baker; an interesting character. He purchased the advowson (an ecclesiastical term which means a right of presentation to a vacant benefice), of Batcombe and Upton Noble in 1878. He engaged the architect Robert Jewell Withers (1823–1894), a prolific builder and restorer of churches who was renowned for converting barn-like structures into something artistically worthy. According to Pevsner, there are three churches in Dorset with which he was connected, St Nicholas, Hilfield (1848), St Andrew, Leigh and, very likely, St Mary, Melbury Bubb. Withers wrote to the Diocesan Registrar the same year, 1878, describing the decayed building. He drew up plans to restore, rebuild and enlarge the church which were accepted. With all the enlargements over the centuries, one can only imagine how small the original had been; it is still tiny. The total cost of building the church amounted to £1,000, the Revd.Baker donating £300, plus a further £220 guarantee. The balance was raised locally. Unfortunately the Revd Baker eventually went bankrupt his consolation being that he was thanked and rewarded for his rebuilding, and for his share of the cost, by the donation of a silver flagon to the church in 1880, in his name.

The roofs of both nave and chancel are barrel-vaulted; the chancel E. window of 1878 by Clayton and Bell *(see Silton)*; the chancel floor covered with typical red and black Victorian encaustic tiles. Glazed earthenware floor tiles were introduced during the medieval period in the twelfth century. From 1835 Victorian encaustic tiles are often found in churches, particularly those which have undergone a Gothic Revival restoration. Herbert Minton was one of the foremost producers of this type of tile. Whereas medieval tiles were handmade and show characteristics of individuality the encaustic, being mass-produced, are uniform and exact. Encaustic (burnt in) is achieved by stamping a design into a plain clay tile, whilst it is still damp, before firing and then filling the impression with liquid clay of a contrasting colour. Firing fuses the two together. From 1850 a clear glazed finish was adopted and from 1860 a wide range of colours began to be used on single tiles. Victorian tiles usually carried the makers name on the reverse side.

Both the Norman period tub font and the pulpit, in a fifteenth-century style are, in fact, perfect in and for their setting. Particular attention is drawn to three fine carvings believed to have been made some time shortly after 1945 for St Paul's Cathedral, London; one, of two angels supporting an escutcheon bearing the monogram of Jesus – IHS; the other two, depicting angels bearing scrolls with latin texts. It would appear that no explanation can be given for the fact that these carvings are now at Upton Noble.

It is predominantly Revd Baker's restoration which the visitor can enjoy today. The cleric, Robert Skinner, in a sermon preached before King Charles I at Whitehall in 1634, declared that the purpose of a church is a, ' … place where our Lord God most holy doth inhabit, His proper mansion or dwelling house.' Whether Whitehall or Upton Noble, the same article of faith still prevails. It is wonderful to sit quietly in this lovely, simple building, so well cared for now; let the centuries unwind and mentally try to recapture the decay, the frustration and the bitterness of those eighteenth and nineteenth-century parishioners who could see this rural gem, their St Mary Magdalene, falling apart before their eyes for lack of care and concern. Small, simple and rustic; heavy in history.

WITHAM FRIARY
– East Somerset

South-west of Frome, off the B3092.
O.S.Landranger 183.

Dedicated to the Blessed Virgin Mary, Saint John Baptist and All Saints

Should the visitor feel a surge of architectural adrenalin, after recently discovering Bruton and Batcombe fairly close by, he or she will be somewhat dismayed upon arriving in Witham. No superb tower here only a simple three-belled cot at the W. end with the ropes visibly coursing down the wall disappearing into a lean-to construction. The visitor might then easily be tempted to move on at this point but the flying buttresses and an apsidal E. end may cause the now curious stranger to take a quick look around.

Having obtained the church key, as instructed on the church notice board, and entered the lean-to building, the visitor gazes down the nave. No trace of traditional village church architecture here, indeed is it even English? With the austerity of the interior and the pervading spirituality of the place, which is almost tangible, the informed visitor may even consider that they could be standing in part of a monastic building.

Anyone desiring an in-depth *investigation* – the correct meaning of the Greek word *Historia* – into the Friary background should buy *Witham Friary Church and Parish* by Michael McGarvie FSA published by Frome Society for Local Study, 1989, which is available in the church. It is an essential guide for even the briefest of visits.

The guide book makes those who enter the church aware that they tread upon specially hallowed ground as Witham Friary was once a centre of religious life in England. In fact, there is a direct connection with two of the most prominent figures of the English Medieval Church; Saint Thomas of Canterbury and Saint Hugh of

Lincoln. In 1170 following the murder of Thomas Becket, King Henry II pledged to the Pope that he would found four monasteries as an act of contrition and penance, thereby acknowledging that he was culpable for the death of the Archbishop. He gave the Royal Manor of Witham to the austere Carthusian Order. In 1179, having already had two priors, a third Prior was appointed and so it was that Hugh of Avalon, already known to Henry by reputation of his talents, was dispatched from the monastic mother house, La Grande Chartreuse, some fifteen miles from Grenoble, to take up office at Witham. Hugh was a truly great figure of that period; energetic, perceptive, a great administrator and a man of humour. He had been at Witham for seven years when, in 1186 he left, reluctantly, to become Bishop Hugh of Lincoln. He died in November 1200, having made his last visit to Witham in 1199. On this occasion he decided to stay in the lay brothers' quarters on the final night of his visit. Fire broke out in the kitchen and Hugh went into the chapel to pray for the fire to be extinguished, which it was. Witham Friary Church, as it is now, was the lay brothers' chapel and it was this building which Hugh entered to pray. Hugh was canonised in 1220, thus becoming Saint Hugh of Lincoln.

The guide draws the visitor's attention to the fact that the building, with its ribbed vaulting, reflects the French style which would, of course, have been familiar to Hugh of Avalon. It is a transitional style between heavy Norman, and the burgeoning gracefulness of Early English architecture. The lay brothers' chapel, now the parish church of Witham Friary, is all that remains of a once great Carthusian monastic establishment. The Carthusians were an ascetic order and this their first monastery in England. Following the dissolution of the monasteries by Henry VIII in 1539, a total of five hundred and sixty establishments were suppressed; Witham amongst them.

After absorbing the spiritual ambience of the interior, one becomes aware of the simplicity of the stained-glass in the nave. The medieval glass was re-set to perfection during the mid-Victorian period *c.*1865, within plain glass surrounds by Horwood Bros. of Frome. For admirers of the outstanding work of Sir Ninian Comper there are four windows in the S. side, dedicated in 1923, which illustrate episodes in the life of St Hugh. Sir John Ninian Comper (1864–1960), was, briefly, a pupil of Charles Eamer Kempe between 1881–82 and then articled to the architects Bodley and Garner (1882–87). Comper received some very important commissions which was largely due to his sensitive handling of the subject matter and for his awareness of the final setting for his finished work. Comper's artistic philosophy was 'Christ in Glory' rather than 'Christ Crucified'. He was also in favour of the free standing altar, a radical move, thus breaking away from the Laudian tradition. (Under Archbishop William Laud [1573–1645], the altar had become a chief feature of a church and it had to be firmly placed against the E. wall of a chancel.) Comper was responsible for building fifteen churches and the restoration of numerous others; Anglican and Roman Catholic. His artistic contribution is spread wide throughout our nation's churches and cathedrals and he is rightly most famous for the Warrior Chapel in Westminster Abbey. Comper designed the exquisite St Cyprian's Church, Clarence Gate, London in 1902, but his finest and richest creation is St Mary's, Wellingborough, Northants., the church where he wanted to be buried. His wish was not granted, however, as he was interred in Westminster Abbey. The four windows here at Witham are sublime examples of Sir Ninian's artistry. *(See also East Knoyle.)*

The present E. window in the Early English style is comprised of three lancets, the centre light depicting *Christ in Majesty*. The window is in memory of Revd C G R Festing. The present glass was dedicated in 1909, after the original glass perished.

The Friary formerly had a conventional W. tower, built during the Georgian period. A major restoration was undertaken in 1875 when new W. end bays were added. During this reconstruction the tower was demolished and in its foundations an elegant fifteenth-century font was discovered where it had been discarded during the earlier Georgian restoration of 1828. It was, as can be seen, rescued, restored and re-placed in situ.

The exterior walls are supported by ten elegant flying buttresses, copied from Lincoln Cathedral, which were added in 1875 to support the insecure foundations as the walls were being pushed from their upright.

There are numerous internal and external features of the fabric to be appreciated including interior furnishings and memorials of great quality. Witham Friary is a church which deserves a greater appreciation in a much wider sphere. It is a building not only of outstanding but simple beauty and spirituality, it is also significant in the development of Christianity in England.

WYKE CHAMPFLOWER
– East Somerset

South-west of Bruton.
O.S.Landranger 183.

Dedicated to
the Holy Trinity

Although a parish church
Holy Trinity, in size, is
more like a chapel with
no spire or tower. It was built in 1623, during the Jacobean period but
with windows and doorways in the Gothic Perpendicular tradition.
This was not unusual as churches continued to be built in the
conservative Gothic style until just prior to the Restoration of 1660, and
occasionally beyond, with a revival of Gothic in the Victorian period.

The church notes refer to Wyke Champflower as a small hamlet set
under Creech Hill. A 'wyke' was a dairy farm and one Luke de
Champflower is recorded as holding the Manor in 1166. It is still very
much a farming community with a current population of around one
hundred, only a few more than the ninety-three of 1831, when there
were fewer buildings. Wyke Champflower has always been a chapelry
to Bruton and it still identifies with the town in parochial affairs.

Holy Trinity is not the first church on this site. The first, a twelfth-
century chapel-of-ease, the responsibility of the Prior of Bruton, was
dedicated to St Michael. Subsequently, in 1482, it was rededicated to St
Peter. That edifice fell into a state of disrepair and the present building
was erected in 1623 by the Southworth family, and rededicated in 1624
to the Holy Trinity. In the chancel is a well-proportioned marble tablet
in the Classical style on the S. wall, dedicated to Henry Southworth,
Lord of the Manor, who died in 1625. This tablet was most likely placed
here at a time well beyond 1625, as it bears a strong Renaissance
influence – a rebirth of ideas including classical art and architecture.

Is the church easy to find? Well … Make your way to Bruton and
into the town one-way traffic system, turn left onto the A371 road to

Shepton Mallet. Carry on until you see, on the left, Wyke Farmhouse Cheese Co.Ltd. where you turn left again. Not far beyond the gates of this shrine to Cheddar Cheese making, is a group of farm buildings; large wooden barn etc. Immediately adjacent to these buildings and still on the left, look for a small, unobtrusive finger-post, ' TO THE CHURCH' where there is a small car park. Follow the path on foot.

The larger building, to which the church is so close, is the handsome Wyke Manor (privately owned). It is in fact so close that the church is literally attached to the rear of the Manor. Holy Trinity is, internally, a building of refinement and architectural elegance. Love at first sight? Most definitely! Church, manor house and approach is a splendid, unified ensemble.

Every aspect of the church's form is architecturally understated; externally and internally, which accords perfectly with the domestic architecture of the Manor. Access to the exterior is limited, due to the S. side of the church abutting the Manor property and the W. end directly annexed to the house. The external walls are rendered; the original rubble or ashlar blocks beneath would have been far preferable. The totally contrasting N. porch entrance of honey-coloured Ham Hill stone is sharply defined and the spandrels of the architrave are delicately worked. In place of a tower is a small, elaborate bell-cot, scaled to the rest of the building.

As the church is not permanently open, instructions on how to obtain the key, and the times and regularity of Divine Service, are displayed in the porch. Before passing into the nave, note the almost four-centuries-old, iron-studded door and the entrance, again in Ham Stone; its simple spandrels sharp and unweathered lovingly crafted by a stonemason of so long ago. Run your fingers over the motifs, which is most likely what the mason did, with pride and affection, when they were finished.

Jacobean furnishing style makes its impact in the interior. For such a small building, of around forty-six feet in length, it is filled with period furnishings which will enchant and delight; especially lovers of fine craftsmanship in wood. There is dark oak panelling to dado level around all four walls and superbly patinated box pews with doors, on both sides of the centre aisle. Take a seat, hang your hat on the wall pegs and imbibe the atmosphere. It is within these small and intimate churches that one can feel the presence of former churchgoers more powerfully; passing to and fro in elegant period clothing. They are still here; the bonnets and bustles, modesty vests and vestments, watch-chains and waistcoats …

Arching above all is a gem of a coved ceiling, made more attractive by the painted armorial shields on the intersecting joints of the timbers. The only overstated feature in the entire building is the large pulpit, not of carved wood as one might expect, but of Portland stone. Nevertheless it is in an unmistakable Jacobean style with crisply carved detailed strapwork and foliage. It now leans at an angle and has developed a profusion of cracks, but not so large that they detract from the pulpit's dignity and elegance. It is believed that it was brought to Holy Trinity from elsewhere; whence is unknown but it was here at the re-dedication in 1624. (From 1603, the year of Elizabeth I's death, all churches were obliged to have a pulpit). Whilst noting the large pulpit one might miss the original carved oak Jacobean font cover on the modern font which is traditionally sited at the W. end of the church. Separating the nave from the chancel is a wooden screen, or tympanum, secured to the ceiling. In the centre is painted the royal arms of King James I dated 1624, on the left are the arms of Arthur Lake, Bishop of Bath and Wells and on the right those of George Abbot, Archbishop of Canterbury from 1611 to 1633.

To shine a metaphorical spotlight on the royal arms and those of George Abbot, Archbishop of Canterbury is to illuminate an interesting corner of English history. To see royal arms in churches, painted either on to boards (the most conventional) or directly onto the walls, is a common sight. (The Arms of the Roman Catholic Mary I are very rarely seen, whilst those of Elizabeth I are relatively numerous). This continued in the early Stuart period and it was George Abbot in 1614 who authorised a painter-stainer to conduct a survey and paint, in all churches and chapels in the Realm of England, the king's arms , with helmet, crest, mantle and supporters, together with the arms of the noble young princes.

George Abbot, in 1631, again instructed that royal arms should be painted and repaired, together with the Ten Commandments and other holy sentences. Boards with the Decalogue are to be found in many churches, placed in a prominent position, usually on the walls. Here at Holy Trinity such a board is to be found placed above the altar, behind the Crucifix. The E. window above the altar is of three lights; the centre light displays fragments of glass, possibly fifteenth-century, depicting the royal arms. The left light shows the Prince of Wales' feathers. The feathers badge is the device of the heir apparent to the English throne. The future Charles I, son of James I (VI of Scotland), was created Prince of Wales in 1616. The right hand light bears the arms of Elizabeth, daughter of James I (sister of Charles I). Elizabeth married Frederick V, Elector Palatine of the Rhine, the leading Calvinist Prince of Germany. It was George Abbot, as Archbishop, who promoted the marriage of Elizabeth to Frederick, but it was also Abbot who resisted the idea of a marriage between the Prince of Wales and the Catholic Spanish Infanta. Abbot was probably the leading Calvinist in England during these years and by promoting one Royal marriage and resisting another he attempted to ensure that Protestantism was firmly established in England and that Catholicism had no fertile ground in which to flourish. These painted boards and stained and painted glass windows are a small insight into what was taking place in England between church and state during the years prior to and following Holy Trinity being considered and built. Holy Trinity was reconsecrated in 1624 and the large church bible which was used at that service is housed in a glass-topped cabinet by the pulpit. Examining this simple display one is reminded that the past is not a different place. Nearly four hundred years divide ourselves from the people of that time but the message proclaimed by the bible unites us all.

In the eloquent words of the compiler of the church notes, on behalf of The Society of Friends of Wyke Champflower:

It is a building with its own sense of time, scarcely changed to the eye since built and unchanging in purpose. Perhaps more than anything it is the peaceful simplicity of the place that remains a lasting memory of a visit.

BIBLIOGRAPHY

PRIMARY SOURCES

Bede, (tr.Shereley-Price,Leo) *Ecclesiastical History of the English People*: Penguin, 1955.

Fiennes,Celia, (ed.Christopher Morris) *Journeys of Celia Fiennes*: Webb & Bower, (Michael Joseph), 1982.

Florence of Worcester, (tr.Stevenson,Revd Joseph, MA) *The Church Historians of England*: Seeleys, 1853.

Florentii Wigorniensis, (tr.Thorpe,Benjamin) *Chronicon Ex Chronicis, Tomus I*: Sumptibus Societatis, 1848.

King Edward II, *Calendar of the Close Rolls for the Reign of Edward II AD1307–1313*: London, 1892.

—— *Calendar of the Close Rolls for the Reign of King Edward II AD1313–1318*: London,1893.

King Edward III, *Calendar of the Close Rolls for the Reign of King Edward III AD1330–1333*: London, 1898.

King William I, (tr.Alecto Historical) *Domesday Book*: Penguin, 2003.

Royal Commission on Historical Monuments, *Historical Monuments in the County of Dorset*: HMSO, 1972.

JOURNALS

The Journal of the British Society of Master Glass Painters, 1927 pp 87–94 Rackham,Bernard, *English Importations of Foreign Stained Glass in the Early Nineteenth Century.*

The Builder, No.27 November 1847, p 565: *Church Building* (Sutton Waldron).

Secondary Sources

Allen,Frank J., *The Great Church Towers of England*: Cambridge University Press, 1932.

Betjeman,John(ed), *Parish Churches of England and Wales*: Collins, 1960.

Chadwick,Owen, *The Victorian Church Vols I & II*: A.& C.Black , 1966 & 1970.

Child,Mark, *Discovering Church Architecture*: Shire Pubs.Ltd., 1976.

Claydon,Anthony, *The Nature of Knoyle*: The Hobnob Press, 2002.

Clifton-Taylor,Alec, *English Parish Churches as Works of Art*: B.T.Batsford Ltd., 1974.

Dickinson,J.C., *An Ecclesiastical History of England – The Later Middle Ages*: A. & C.Black, 1979.

Dirsztay,Patricia, *Inside Churches*: NADFAS, 1993.

Dodd,Dudley, *Stourhead*: National Trust, 1997.

Draper,Jo, *Dorset, the Complete Guide*: The Dovecote Press, 1986.

Durant,David N., *The Handbook of British Architectural Styles*: Barrie & Jenkins, 1992.

Fines,John, *History from the Sources – The Domesday Book in the Classroom*: Phillimore & Co., 1982.

Frere,Sheppard, Britannia – *A History of Roman Britain*: Routledge & Kegan Paul, 1976.

Friar,Stephen, *Heraldry*: Sutton Pub., 1992.

Gooder,Eileen A, *Temple Balsall: the Warwickshire preceptory of the Templars and their fate*: Phillimore & Co., 1995.

Harries,John,(rev.Hicks,Carola), *Discovering Stained Glass*: Shire Pubs., 2001.

Harrison,Martin, *Victorian Stained Glass*: Barrie & Jenkins, 1980.

Hawkins,Desmond, *Cranborne Chase*: The Dovecote Press, 1980.

Hoare,Sir R.C., *History of Modern Wiltshire*: 1822–1844.

Howe,Charles, *Gylla's Hometown*: Gylla Publishing, 1983.

Hutchings,Monica, *Inside Dorset*: The Abbey Press, 1965.

Hutchins,John, *The History and Antiquities of the County of Dorset. Vols.III & IV*: 1868, Rep.EP Publishing Ltd., 1973.

Jenkins,Simon, *England's Thousand Best Churches*: Penguin, 2000.

Little,Joyce, *Stained Glass Marks and Monograms*: NADFAS, 2002.

Mattingly,Harold, *Roman Imperial Civilisation*: Edward Arnold Ltd., 1957.

Nicholson,Helen, *The Knights Templar*: Sutton Publishing, 2001.

—— *The Trial of the Templars in the British Isles*: (forthcoming).

O'Malley,Greg, *The Knights Hospitaller of the English Langue 1460–1565*: OUP (forthcoming).

Ottewell,Gordon, *Literary Strolls in Wiltshire and Dorset*: Sigma Leisure, 2002.

Pevsner,Nicholas, *Buildings of England – Dorset*: Penguin, 1972.

—— *Buildings of England – North Somerset and Bristol*: Penguin, 1958.

—— *Buildings of England – West Somerset*: Penguin, 1958.

—— *Buildings of England – Wiltshire*: Penguin, 1963.

Pitt-Rivers,General Augustus H., *Excavations in Cranborne Chase. IV Vols*: 1887–98.

Pugh,R.B.(ed), *The Victoria History of the Counties of England – Wiltshire Vol.I*: O.U.P., 1957.

—— **& Crittell,E.**(eds), *The Victoria History of the Counties of England – Wiltshire Vol.II*: O.U.P., 1955.

Raguin,Virginia Chieffo, *The History of Stained Glass*: Thames & Hudson Ltd., 2003.

Riley-Smith,Jonathan, *Hospitallers – The History of the Order of St John*: Hambledon Press, 1999.

—— (ed), *The Oxford History of the Crusades*: O.U.P., 1999.

Romanelli,Giandomenico (ed), *Venice Art and Architecture*: Könemann, 1997.

Sawyer,Rex, *A History of the Parish Church of St John the Baptist, Tisbury*: 1999.

Shreeves,Bill, *King's Court Gillingham*: Gillingham Museum, 2002.

Stavridi,Margaret, *Master of Glass Charles Eamer Kempe 1837–1907*: The Kemp Society, 1988.

Stenton,Sir Frank, *Anglo-Saxon England*: O.U.P., 1971.

Swanton,Michael (ed.), *The Anglo-Saxon Chronicles*: Phoenix Press, 2000.

Taylor,Richard, *How to Read a Church*: Rider, 2003.

Tinniswood,Adrian, *His Invention So Fertile (Sir Christopher Wren)*: Jonathan Cape, 2001.

Trevor-Roper, Hugh, *Archbishop Laud*: Macmillan, 1940.

Wagner,A.F.H.V., *The Church of St Mary the Virgin Gillingham*: Blackmore Press, 1956.

Weaver,J.R.H., *The Chronicle of John of Worcester*: Clarendon Press, 1908.

Wheeler,Mortimer, *Archaeology from the Earth*: O.U.P., 1954.

Wickham,A.K., *Churches of Somerset*: Phoenix House, 1952.

Wilson,A.N., *The Victorians*: Hutchinson, 2002.

Wrigley,Chris, *William Barnes – The Dorset Poet*: Dovecote Press Ltd., 1984.

GLOSSARY

Apse – A semi-circular or polygonal end to a chancel. Could also be used to describe a similar shaped chapel extending beyond the walls of the main building. Because of the apse shape, it is often vaulted.

Architrave – Main beam which rests on a capital or the moulding around arches, doorways or windows.

Art Nouveau – *c*.1900 Florid floral decoration originating in the later Victorian and Edwardian period. Much loved style in church carving of panels etc.

Ashlar – Dressed and squared stone blocks of varying size; smooth faced, fitted and joined together. Could be of a large face area, but not necessarily thick. Often used in exterior walls to surface coarser masonry behind.

Ball flower – Globular flower of three petals which enclose a small ball.

Base – The lowest section of a column or a pier between the shaft and the ground.

Battlements – Indented wall above a tower or nave roof.

Bell Capital – The headstone of a column. Shaped so that it appears like an upturned bell.

Benefice – A church living.

Blank or Blind Clerestory – Formed by extending the wall of the nave above an aisle roof without the addition of windows.

Boss – Ornament carved, or otherwise, placed at an intersection in a roof or a vault to hide the joining points.

Brass – Brass sheet memorial in the likeness of a dead person to whom it is dedicated. Usually inlaid into a stone surround or slab.

Broach – Octagonal spire rising from the top of a tower, the triangular space at each angle of the tower is filled in by masonary inclined from each right-angle.

Capital – Large headstone of a column or pilaster used for supporting arches or ribs, frequently richly carved.

Chancel – An Eastern continuation of a nave. This, conventionally, contains an altar and choir stalls. *(see Sanctuary)*

Chancel Screen – Divides the nave from the chancel. They sometimes have doors.

Chantry Chapel – A small chapel in which Masses are said for the souls of those who endowed it.

Clerestory – A structure which continues the nave wall upwards; with windows to allow more natural light.

Coffered – A decorated, sunken, ceiling panel.

Column – A cylindrical, vertical pillar, usually supporting an arch.

Corbel – A short block, stone or wood, projecting from a wall to act as support for an arch or beam. Can be carved or moulded.

Crocket, Crocketing – Decorative features placed on the sloping sides of spires, pinnacles, gables and the outside of arches etc., usually placed at regular intervals.

Curvilinear tracery – Consisting of or contained by a curved line or lines.

Cusp(ed) – A small projecting point at the intersection of the arc in the tracery of Gothic windows and arches.

Decalogue – The Ten Commandments.

Decorated Period (Dec.) – *c.*1272–1350. English Gothic architecture in its second period. A period which saw the heightening and widening of aisles already in existence. Additions were made in the form of pinnacles, parapets and also porches. Tracery around windows became more ornate.

Dog Tooth – A Norman and Early English form of decoration in a repeat pattern, e.g. around arches and doorways.

Early English Period – *c*.1170–1300. The first period of English Gothic architecture. Lancet windows and pointed arches appear. Beautifully carved foliage and animals. Salisbury Cathedral is of this period.

Engaged Column or Pilaster – Vertical column or a shaft engaged or let into a wall.

Extrados – The outside curve of an arch.

Flying Buttress – An arch bridging two walls or connecting a wall over a roof of an aisle to a main buttress.

Foliate – Carved with leafy ornamentation.

Gable – The verticle triangular piece of a wall at the end of a ridge roof.

Gablets – Small gables, often found around windows.

Garth – A piece of enclosed ground, frequently with a defining word e.g. cloister.

Georgian Period – 1714–1830.

Glebe – A portion of land assigned to a clergyman as part of his benefice.

Gothic Revival – 19th-cent. attempt by architects and designers to hark back to the true Gothic style.

Jacobean Period – James I (1603–25) elaborately carved woodwork; screens, pulpits, lecterns etc. were of particular note during this period.

Lancet Window – Tall and narrow light, sharply pointed.

Lectern – Reading desk to support a usually large Bible. An eagle is a favourite subject for lecterns.

Light – A window for letting in light.

Lucarne or Spire light – Window on the flat surface of a spire.

Lychgate – An entrance, usually covered with a sloping roof, at the entrance to a churchyard. Originally to provide shelter for the coffin whilst waiting for the priest to arrive.

Misericord – A support for a single seat, when it is lifted. These are frequently beautifully carved into grotesque, sacred figures or, sometimes, a subject favoured by the carver.

Nave – Main body of the church in which a congregation of people sit during divine services.

Niche – Plain or ornamental recess set in a wall, its purpose is to house a statue.

Norman Period – *c.*1066–1200. Towers, largely square; impressive and large buildings. Strongly moulded arches and doorways.

Ogee – A double curve bending first one way and then the other.

Parapet – A low wall above the roof or the eaves. Visual effect of breaking the line of a flat roof.

Parclose – A partition, screen or railing in a church enclosing an altar or tomb; or separating a chapel from the main body of the church.

Paten – Plate for the eucharist bread or wafer, usually silver.

Pediment – *(see Tympanum)*

Perpendicular Period (Perp.) – *c.*1350–1539. The third period of English Gothic architecture. Soaring splendour; with lofty proportions, verticals, large windows and high arches.

Pew – Bench type seats with ends, often carved or decorated, some with doors.

Pier – Vertical and freestanding pillar; cylindrical, octagonal or rectangular. Can also be arranged in groups.

Pilaster – *(see engaged column)*

Pinnacle – Vertical turret found at the top of buttresses, roofs, towers etc. Can be decorated with crockets or foliate shapes, the whole tapering to a point or finial.

Piscina – A niche within which is a stone bowl with drain. It is usually found within the chancel sanctuary, and its purpose is for the washing of sacred vessels, e.g. chalice and paten, after use. Double piscina can sometimes be found, as in Witham Friary, their function is, one for washing hands and the other for washing vessels, as above.

Putto (*pl.***Putti**) – Latin – *putus* boy. Representations of small children used in art.

Quatrefoil – Tracery shaped in the form of a four section leaf pattern; frequently used in windows, carvings etc. *(see Trefoil)*

Rebus – A pictorial pun on a name.

Reformation – A major revolution in religion in the 16th cent. which rejected the Pope as Supreme head of the Christian church. The result of the turmoil was the beginning of the Protestant church.

Renaissance Period – *c.*1485–1689. Italian in origin, which influenced English church architecture.

Reredos – Decorated Screen which could be wood, stone, tapestry or painted; situated behind the altar. A background to the altar to give the sacred table a focus.

Rood or Holy Rood – The Cross of Christ. Sometimes with figures and often fitted on the top level of the Rood Screen.

Rood Screen – wooden or stone carved screen separating the nave from the choir.

Sanctuary – The area surrounding the altar, beyond the altar rails.

Saxon Period – *c.*600–1066. The Saxon church in Bradford-on-Avon, Wiltshire is a survivor of this period.

Sedila or Sedillia – Recessed seats in niches, usually in the S. wall of the chancel, used by the clergy. Can be decorated and canopied; stone or wood.

Spandrel – A triangular space between the outer curve of an arch and the rectangle formed by the mouldings enclosing it.

Stained Glass – Painted pieces of glass held together in a lead framework.

Stair Turret – Enclosed stairway to the ringing-stage of a tower. To be found with either internal or external doors to gain access to the bells. Some turrets are extended beyond the top of the tower. Can be an elegant addition to a tower.

String course – A stone course or moulding projecting from the surface of a wall.

Tracery – Ornamental stonework in a window, screen or panels.

Transitional Period – *c.*1150–1200. Late Norman.

Trefoil – Tracery in the form of a three sectioned, stylised leaf; used in windows, carvings etc. *(see Quatrefoil)*

Tudor Period – *c.*1485–1603. Late Perpendicular.

Tympanum – Space between the lintel at the top of a doorway and the arch above. Often contains sculpture in high or low relief. Characteristic of Norman architecture.

Vault – Underground area for burials.

Vaulting – Arched roof, ceiling or arch-like structures, with ribs radiating from a central point.

INDEX